BLOOM WHERE YOU'RE PLANTED

DAILY ADVENTURES IN SELF INSPIRATION

JACQUES WIESEL

Holocaust Survivor

Copyright © 2019 by Jacques Wiesel.

ISBN		Softcover		978-1-948801-74-4

All rights reserved. No part of this book may be reproduced or transmitted in any form or by any means, electronic or mechanical, including photocopying, recording, or by any information storage and retrieval system without express written permission from the author, except in the case of brief quotations embodied in critical reviews and certain other non-commercial uses permitted by copyright law.

Printed in the United States of America.

To order additional copies of this book, contact:
Bookwhip
1-855-339-3589
https://www.bookwhip.com

To my wife Carole Wiesel,
whose heart is bigger than her body
and who teaches me daily
what love is truly all about.

Contents

POSITIVE THOUGHTS FOR A BETTER LIFE 1

Getting Rid of Past Memories 2
2 B or Not 2 B 3
Walk Your Talk 4
Motivation 5
Setting Goals 6
UPS Calling 8
Life Is a Boomerang 9
Just What the Doctor Ordered 10
Nature 11
Faultfinders 12
On Race Relations 14
PARENTS 15
Carpe Diem 16
Pessimism 17
Trance-Formation 18
Where Are You Going? 20
Procrastination 21
Problem-Project 22
Pre-Game Strategy 23
The Superbawl 24
The 10 Forgettables 26
Value-Added 27
Selling Yourself 28

A MONTH FOR EXPANDING THE HEART 29

Forgiveness 30
Prescription for Life 31

Patience 33
The Key 34
Mirror, Mirror on the Wall 35
A Tip for Non-Tippers 36
In-Laws 37
TLC 39
Options from Within 40
Loving Yourself 41
Front to Back 42
On Listening 43
Puppy Love 45
ESP 46
Dress Rehearsal 47
The New Commandments 48
Manners 49
The Ties That Bind 51
Show and Tell 52
The Change Quotient 53

MARCH YOURSELF INTO POSITIVE ENERGY 54
Goldfish 55
All the News Unfit to Print 56
Bloom Where You're Planted 58
The Ultimate Oxymoron 59
Combat or Comfort? 60
Another Oxymoron 61
Problems 62
Sex 64
Rent-a-Life 65
Why Clone That Clone? 66
Bagels 67
How to Succeed at Business 68
Fall and Win 70

No "Ifs" 71
Death Row Woman 72
Breaking 100 73
Space 74
The Brain 76
Reunion 77
Symphony of Life 78
Fear of Success 79
Bumper Stickers 80

LIVING FOR YOUR DREAMS 82
April Fool 83
Flaunt Your MBA 84
Time 85
Are Goals Enough? 86
Happiness 87
Peace 89
Blueprints for Life 90
Cleanup Time 91
Accept What You Expect 92
Endowments 93
Pancakes 95
Going Bust 96
Licenses 97
40th Anniversary 98
In Defense of Fruitcake 99
Artificial Intelligence 101
POM Button 102
Apathy 103
Weather 104
Jackdaws 105
Snails and Peaches 107
Smoking 108

MAY YOU BLOOM WHERE YOU ARE PLANTED 109
No Tomorrow 110
This Is Progress? 111
Pet Peeves 112
I Miss the Young Me 114
Ban the Ban 115
DMS and MMS 116
Tears 117
Pro Bono 118
You Can't Go Home Again 120
Unweaving Baskets 121
Halfway 122
2,500 Years of Self-Help 123
Dead Right 124
Mother's Day 126
POW! 127
Birthday Boy 128
Discomfort Zone 129
How's Your PC? 130
Writing 132
News 133
Generation Chasm 134
TV or Not TV 135
Sex and Statistics 136

A ROSE BY ANY OTHER NAME… 137
Roses 139
Negative Faith 140
The Gap 141
Singles 142
Toilet Paper 143
Suicide 145
Wishbone or Backbone 146

Plague 147
55 mph or Bust 148
Terminal Boredom 149
A Job Is a Job Is a Job 151
Generation Gap 152
Odd Couples 153
MYOB 154
The Cosmic Chef 155
Robotics 157
Dark-Light 158
Love and Positive Thinking 159
What Goes Around Comes Around 160
Universal Laws 161

HOT STUFF 163
The Red Phone 164
Faith 165
Hate 166
Independence 167
Something to Chew On 168
Prayer 170
Right v. Right 171
Do You Have an NBA? 172
Excuses 173
Rewards of Reading 174
E Is for Einstein 176
Memories 177
Aspirin 178
Lost Instructions 179
Fireflies 180
Repent Now 182
Early Birds 183
The Circus 184
The Best 185

Join the PGA 186
Miscommunication 188
Action v. Inaction 189
Turn the Other Cheek 190

OVERCOMING OBSTACLES 191

Time Is Short 192
Letting Go 193
Problems 195
The Great Family Hoax 196
Tele-Manners 197
Affirmations 198
No Free Lunch 199
Expectations 201
Dead Poet's Society 202
Altus 203
UFO 204
Success or Failure? 205
Humane Relations 207
The Full Life 208
Image 209
Foot-in-Mouth Disease 210
The Natural 211
Ancient Wisdom 213
GRRRR… 214
Synergy 215
PSI 216
Diving into Work 217

SPRING BACK, FALL AHEAD 219

No Rest for the Weary 220
Risk Your Way to Success 221
Judge Not 222

Three Rs 223
Rest in Peace 224
Horoscopes 226
Kinesics 227
Problem Solvers 228
A Tale of Two Monks 229
The Ego and the Cosmos 230
The Dead Zone 232
Begin at the Beginning 233
Born a Winner, Died a Whiner 234
Three Giants 235
Tasks 236
Where Are You? 238
I'm Okay, You're Okay 239
Educare 240
NLP Revisited 241
Sounds of Love 242
Tuna 244

STORM WARNINGS 245
Stretch Marks 246
Brainwashing 247
A Kinder, Gentler Time 248
Polyticks 249
School 251
48 Hours 252
Our Ps and Rs 253
People Classifier 254
Dinosaurs 255
Bumped 257
Body Betrayal 258
Spiritual Poverty 259
Networking for Success 260
Self-Criticism 261

Taking Inventory 263
Being 264
A Happy Funeral? 265
Satisfaction Guaranteed 266
Ancient Truths 267
Bias 269
Amazing Americans 270
Left and Right 271
Fear 272

THANK GOD, PRAISE YOURSELF 273
Marathon 274
Laughter 276
GOD 277
Love Yourself 278
Psychobabble 279
Neighbors 280
When More Is Less 282
1,000 Points of Light 283
Work 284
Respect 285
I Go, Therefore I Am 286
Power Words 288
Intalk 289
Prosperity 290
Polarity and Synergy 291
Responsibility 292
College Chaos 294
Sacred and Profane 295
Turkey Day 296
Giving Thanks 297
Batteries Not Included 298

GIFTS FROM THE HEART 300
Life's a Bitch 301
Nothing and Everything 302
4-Fs 303
Planned Obsolescence 304
The Ages of Mankind 305
Death Grip 307
Peeping Toms 308
The Pessimist and the Optimist 309
George's Advice 310
Attitude 311
The G Spot 313
The Power of Music 314
Visualize and Vitalize 315
Why Me? 316
The Science of Sex 317
Compromise 319
Self-Love 320
GUS 321
Wherever I Go, Ego! 322
Time for Review 323
Love and Positive Thinking 325
What I Have Learned 326

About the Author 328
Photo Gallery 329

Acknowledgments

I would like to express my sincerest gratitude to the following individuals for their contributions to my life and work:

My friend, Russell Q. Graichen Jr., who has stood by me through thick and thin over the past 20 years as I learned many of the lessons that comprise this book.

My editor, L. A. Justice, who turned my sometimes garbled script into an eminently readable, and I trust enjoyable, feast for the eyes and soul.

My publishers, Peter Vegso and Gary Seidler of Health Communications, whose confidence in this project has made this book a reality.

Introduction

This book took a lifetime to write, yet required only 260 days to put on paper. When I first began to jot down my impressions of the lessons I have learned, and continue to learn, I thought a one-page paper would do. Before I realized what had happened, 600 vignettes had poured out of me via my word processor.

As a professional motivational speaker I am constantly looking for ideas to use in my lectures and seminars, but much of my writing is from the heart and the gut.

As a refugee from World War II, my childhood was far from "normal." As I often tell my audiences, my self-esteem was lower than a centipede with fallen arches. As I matured I began to realize that self-love is the first step to healthy living—both mentally and physically. And so I embarked on a mission to help myself first. Only when I felt I had achieved a degree of self-confidence did I venture to share my experiences on living a healthful life with others. This has now become my mission and I have been able to reach thousands (hopefully millions) through lectures, writings and discs.

The bottom line to my lectures is: If Jacques can do it, you can too.

How to Use This Book

At my lectures I tell my audiences that they are invited to join me at a "cafeteria of ideas." Instead of giving them "food for thought," I offer "thought for food."

In this annual manual, the same idea holds true.

Read before or after breakfast so your day can begin with energy gleaned from the greatest wisdom of the ages—from ancient to modern.

Since your early morning mindset will influence the kind of day you will have, it is important to program yourself on a positive note. Start the day on the right foot.

*Positive
Thoughts for
a Better Life*

Getting Rid of Past Memories

Most childhood memories are mental echoes of negative experiences. Most of them belong in the dust bin. I learned the hard way that most memories hurt like hell.

My earliest schooling, in Brussels, Belgium, where I was born, was run by Catholic nuns who constantly smacked my left hand trying to force me to become right-handed. They considered left-handedness a "crime" against nature. I also recall a lay teacher in Brussels who punished students by inserting their index finger in a bird cage. This sadist forced them to keep it there until the big blackbird pecked at it and drew blood.

In Casablanca, Morocco, the Arab teacher used a cat-o'-nine-tails to keep us in order. Finally, in a parochial school in Brooklyn, the rabbi used a heavy ruler across our knuckles when we did not learn our lessons fast enough, or at his desired level of accuracy.

And I thought learning was supposed to be fun!

The psychologist, Dr. Maxwell Maltz, said we spend 60 percent of our waking hours dwelling on the past. The past is over, yet we cling to it as though it were a life preserver. When we live in the past, we allow the bad feelings to drag us down and keep us operating at a low level of achievement instead of letting good feelings shore up our sagging self-esteem.

The new year is an excellent time to change our act and think of positive solutions to life rather than letting old negative feelings prevail.

Instead of reinforcing negative energy, turn it around and let it propel you into a better future by releasing unpleasant childhood memories. Allow them to come up, play them out in your mind, then send them into outer space. If they come back, turn your thoughts to a positive experience. Defuse the negative and substitute the positive.

Your good past empowers you.

Today—the first day of the new year—is the best time to start.

Go for it!

2 B or Not 2 B

Shakespeare's classic expression, "To be or not to be," takes on more significance now than ever before. In order to understand its current importance, here's an alternate question for you: "Who am I?"

Did you answer with one of the following?

I'm just a sales clerk; I'm only a housewife; I'm simply the janitor; I'm merely the bookkeeper; I'm but a small fish in a big pond; my job is hardly worth talking about; I'm nothing more than a glorified secretary.

While there is nothing wrong with any of those occupations, by answering with a "just," "only," "merely," you demean your position. When you think in this manner, you accept your self-image as "nothing more than." It means you have decided to go through life thinking your talents are not coordinated with your capabilities—making you a victim of circumstance.

Each of us has unlimited potential as God's most important creation. Instead of accepting your lot in life as it is, look at the word "impossible" in a more imaginative fashion. Try seeing it as I. M. Possible.

If you are "just" a sales clerk, why not aim for being the manager? If you are "nothing more" than a glorified secretary, why not set a goal of being the boss? If you're "but" a little fish in a big pond, find a smaller pond, thus becoming a bigger fish!

The world is a large place; expand your horizons. If you take a positive approach to what you can be, instead of what you have become, the brass ring is yours for the grabbing.

Walk Your Talk

"Walk your talk," said my father many years ago.

By that I believe he meant that I should make sure my actions followed my words.

As an adult I have seen that too many of us are locked into the philosophy of "say one thing and do another." When we act in this manner we confuse our own reasoning as well as those of others.

Ever run a red light, then lean over to Junior and say, "Do as I say, not as I do"? Same thing. Everyone is baffled. Why is it okay for you, but not Junior when he drives?

Likewise, our credibility is lowered when one set of rules applies to one group or one individual and another set of rules applies to the rest.

You are the boss. You have No Smoking signs posted, yet you are allowed to light up. Why is it okay for you and not for your employees? How can they respect you and your judgment when you flaunt your authority?

Say what you mean, even if it means you don't say much. Then follow through. Life is much simpler when you obey this simple rule. Everyone around you will know that you will "walk your talk" and, hopefully, they'll follow your example.

Motivation

New college graduates were asked to define their number-one problem as they prepared for their entry into the outside business world. Three out of four answered with the same words: self-confidence.

A lack of self-confidence equals a poor self-image, as well as low self-esteem. A weak learning foundation, combined with a non nurturing home environment, eventually lead to low personal motivation. In this society, high expectations and a high sense of self are crucial elements to success in life.

It's been said that where there is life there is hope and this holds true for motivation.

A timeless article in *Reader's Digest,* based on a 25-year study at Harvard University, confirms the fact that if we change how we think about ourselves, as well as our surroundings, we can redirect motivation and improve performance.

If a new graduate wants to go to a job interview with a positive outlook (and who doesn't?), an attitude adjustment is sometimes necessary. I have found the best method is to replace the old way of thinking with a new philosophy that will brighten the immediate future.

How does one do that?

There are many ways. I suggest reading the classic books, which will give you a foundation in good literature; read biographies of famous people and you will see that many of them overcame tremendous obstacles. Wilma Rudolph, the Olympic gold medal sprinter, had polio as a child and was told she would never walk!

Attend motivational seminars and listen to empowerment tapes. There are many other avenues that will help change your self-esteem from low to high, from negative to positive.

According to the Dale Carnegie Foundation, job aptitude accounts for 15 percent of our success while mental attitude accounts for 85 percent!

Accept the fact that you are born to win and you will win. You will take positive action to achieve your goal, however high it may be. The sky is the limit.

Setting Goals

Now is a good time to find out exactly who you are and what you want out of life. Answer these questions with one of the following: Happy, Content, Unhappy.

1. How do you feel about your current financial situation?
2. Your job/occupation?
3. Your family life?
4. Yourself?

If you are unhappy with most of them, you need to spend some time rethinking your goals and perhaps setting them at a higher level.

If you are content with those four aspects of your life, you probably need to push yourself into something more rewarding. If you are happy, you are a lucky person. Few of us are really happy with our lives. Take a more careful look. Are you being honest? If so, congratulations. Now dig a little deeper.

A. What do you admire most about yourself?
B. What do you dislike about yourself?
C. Are you satisfied with your current level of success?
D. Do you feel appreciated by your peers?
E. Do you think your problems are caused by other people's attitudes, or yours?
F. If you could change any part of your life what would it be?
G. How much would you like to earn next year?
H. What would be your first step in attaining this goal?
I. Is your self-esteem high, low or average?
J. Does negative energy hold you back from having a higher sense of self and earning more money?

Generally speaking, past anger, hatreds, frustrations and lack of positive energy hold us back from attaining these goals. Forgive yourself for any past transgressions. Today is a new day. Begin again.

Take a careful look at your answers. It's an excellent springboard for you to set new and higher goals for yourself.

Once you forgive others and forgive yourself, you take charge of your career by hopping on the "success express."

*"We know nothing about motivation.
All we can do is write books about it."*

PETER DRUCKER

*"It takes 20 years to make an
overnight success."*

EDDIE CANTOR

UPS Calling

Are you expecting a delivery truck? Most people, if asked, would say that they are waiting for something to happen. But I've got news for you. If you didn't put in an order, that package won't arrive. What are you sending out which will require a response?

If you put a kettle of water on the stove and wait for it to boil, you'll turn into a skeleton before you hear the whistle blow—if you didn't turn on the power!

Life moves on whether you participate or not. Active and passive participation use up the same amount of time. Doesn't it make sense to use it constructively?

You can sit around waiting for the Grim Reaper to snatch you away, or you can put your time to good use. If you live to be 80, think of the contributions you can make—not only to your own enjoyment of life, but to others as well.

Look at the late George Burns. He made it to age 100. He didn't sit around waiting for the UPS truck to deliver a good life. He went out and made one for himself. You can too.

Moaning that you are bored and that nobody cares about you is the ultimate in negative thinking. Turn that around by setting high goals for each and every day. Even if you don't reach them, they will leave you on a better level of personal achievement than before.

Life Is a Boomerang

What you send out comes back—in one form or another.

If you project anger, either the recipient catches it and flings it back, with interest, or the recipient ducks, leaving your anger to boomerang back at you.

It's a classic scenario of a lose-lose mentality.

If you telegraph a grudge or bad vibes toward someone, you stand a good chance of "eating your words" since universal law dictates that what you give out will be measured back to you with interest.

The trick is to control the boomerang effect. Healthy self-control results from the intelligent use of empathy, compassion and genuine concern for others.

Put otherwise, sweetened words are more digestible. One of the most insidious products of the boomerang effect is the violence on television. Viewers, young and old, are hypnotized by unrelenting negative output. They can no longer discern the difference between fact and fiction, evil and good, right and wrong. They throw back into the world what they have digested subliminally. This is especially true of young people, whose minds have not fully developed.

According to the Center for Continuing Education at the Australian National University, if you watch violence constantly, violence will become a part of your life. It's a very scary thought, especially when you think of what's on television day and night. Add the boomerang effect and the potential for disaster is mind-blowing.

Just What the Doctor Ordered

The majority of Americans go through life containing their anger and frustration. No wonder they succumb to ailments of all kinds—high blood pressure, heart disease, cancer and ulcers. Drug companies are making billions on prescriptions for tranquilizers and other drugs.

With all due respect to doctors, they find it easier to write out a prescription for sedatives than to make house calls or find out exactly what ails us. They have no time, patients are crammed into every nook and cranny of their offices. If they give us 10 minutes of their time, we should feel blessed.

So it's up to us to diagnose what the problem is.

I ask you, if the human body is our Creator's greatest miracle, why does it require thousands of different drugs for proper maintenance?

The ancient Greek philosopher Aeschylus (525-456 B.C.) understood that the body will respond to what's troubling the mind and cause illness.

When you feel unwell, instead of running to the doctor, ask yourself "Who's bothering me?" You'd be surprised at the answer.

Anxiety attacks can resemble heart attacks. Depression mimics the flu.

When you truly love yourself there is rarely a need for drugs or narcotics. I'm not advocating being your own doctor or not seeing a physician if you are ill, but look at your mindset before rushing off to the doc. Maybe you just need to slow down, take a vacation or have some TLC. A hug goes a long way in curing the doldrums.

In fact, I am a firm believer in hugs, not drugs. I call them HUGs, short for Healthy Unconditional Giving. Try it, maybe it'll work for you.

NATURE

I love sitting by my window in the early morning watching the sun stream in through the vertical blinds. The plants on the sill catch my gaze. While they appear not to move, they are, in reality, constantly in flux—the weak leaves turn yellow, droop and die; new ones take their place, unfurling slowly day by day.

Plants take full advantage of their environment, spreading roots and leaves to encompass every available space. Sadly, this blooming does not carry over to the human species.

According to the Stanford University Human Resources Department, humans use only 2 percent of their abilities on a daily basis. Unlike plants, we do not take advantage of our natural gifts and bountiful environment. Instead, most of us work with a fixed set of ideas and rarely, if ever, change the direction of our thinking.

Do you follow a set pattern every day? I'll bet you wake up, brush your teeth, wash your face, eat breakfast—cereal, coffee and toast—the same thing year after year.

How about shaking yourself up? Expand your horizons. Be flexible. Go with the flow.

Like a plant that finds a little space to use constructively, make life more interesting by having something different for breakfast, take another route to work, eat dessert first!

Even better, turn off the television and meditate. Read a book, talk to a friend or your spouse. Play with the kids. Do something you've never done before. Challenge yourself mentally.

The bottom line is that while plants may be fascinating in their own way, they can't do what we can. So instead of being a couch potato or a stuffed tomato, get out of the rut, uproot your sedentary and set-inyour—way habits and make something happen each and every day.

Faultfinders

I was leafing through my well-worn thesaurus looking for a word that would correspond with critic. The definitions led me to faultfinders and to grouch, which also includes: griper, grouser, growler, grumbler, grump, kicker, malcontent, sorehead and sourpuss.

Every morning I meet a group of these gripers, grumblers and grumps at my morning bagel haven. These malcontents come for their daily breakfast which includes coffee, bagels and an informal kind of group therapy.

Their favorite pastime is judging, blaming, faulting, accusing and cursing. They are like a stew of bad feelings.

It is my contention that we should stay away from the stews being brewed by the soreheads of the world. People whose main vocabulary consists of blame, shame, fault, guilt, hate and hurt, who condemn and criticize, must be avoided at all costs.

The only love I detect from this group every morning is the love of arguing and belittling others.

Once I classified the world into two types of people: the gutter dwellers and the sidewalk residents. Those in the gutter spent their entire life trying to pull others down to their level. While those on the sidewalks tried to elevate others to their status. Faultfinders love to wallow in the gutter with their fellow backbiters.

To criticize is to position yourself above the ones you are casting aspersions on.

If, as William James once said, "The essence of genius is knowing what to overlook in others," then I say, "Let us be content to enjoy people and leave judgment elsewhere."

Or, in other words, judge only the way you would want to be judged.

Even more simply put: Don't judge at all. There is a higher law taking care of this for all of us.

"They always say that time changes things, but you actually have to change them yourself."

ANDY WARHOL

On Race Relations

Today is the day this nation celebrates Martin Luther King's birthday. While I have not encountered the prejudice he did, I have my own sad tales to tell.

My family escaped the reign of Nazi terror in 1940 and relocated to a small French village called Villaries. I was only seven years old and had to run home from school every day because my classmates wanted to see my "horns." I can only guess they thought I was from the land of the Devil.

We moved a month later and landed in Casablanca, Morocco, where we stayed as displaced persons for the next two-and-a-half years.

The Arab kids made life a living hell for me and my brother, taunting us because of our light skin and foreign accents.

According to educators who specialize in early childhood disorders, the first five years are the most important attitude-training years. Before children enter kindergarten they have already acquired basic skills, values and a sense of self-worth (which is commonly referred to as self-esteem). Studies have shown that less than 10 percent of the population has adequate self-esteem. For minorities it is even lower.

The factor remaining constant is the home environment. Parents give mixed signals resulting in poor self-esteem, which I believe is the root of racism.

Once children enter the school system, their values, whether acceptable or not, are already in place. So when we expect teachers to counteract bigotry and prejudice, it's like locking up the barn after the horse is stolen.

Our children are like sponges, absorbing the attitudes around the home. Even if we have prejudices (and who among us doesn't?) we should be careful when we voice those prejudices around the house. We may never live in a world that is free of bigotry and intolerance, but this is as good a time as any to try.

PARENTS

I love to use acronyms, since they make my lectures easier. These mnemonic devices are used for improving the memory. Each letter stands for a word, like SAT is short for Scholastic Aptitude Test.

One of my favorite acronyms is PARENTS and it goes like this:

P is for Patience without which all is lost when communicating with tots. "P" is also for Praise, which we give too little of.

A is for Appreciation with which you should not be skimpy. Apply liberally and watch the wondrous results. A is also for Attitude, which makes life easy (when you go with the flow) or hard (when you fight it).

R is for Respect which you must have for your offspring, no matter how young or old they are. Likewise, they will show you the same—but it must be earned by both sides. It cannot be force-fed or it will become distasteful and all sides will suffer.

E is for Enthusiasm which is as catching as a cold, but in a health enhancing way. E is also for the Ego, which needs continuous boosting so your children will grow into fine upstanding adults with a valuable sense of self-worth.

N is for Neutrality which you must show between siblings. Playing favorites only leads to unhappiness, intense rivalry and a family divided by bad feelings.

T is for Time. Make sure to give them enough of your time even though you have important things to do. They will go elsewhere if you don't listen to them and you will lose touch with them.

S is for Stability, Self-esteem, Sincerity and Self-reliance, all of which lead to Successful child rearing.

So, parents, the key to success is to become positive role models for your offspring. You will reap what you sow; all it takes is patience, appreciation, respect, energy, neutrality, time and sincerity. That's not asking too much, is it?

Carpe Diem

Carpe diem, the Latin phrase for "seize the day," is being spotted all over this great nation of ours. I've seen it on tee shirts, mugs, bumper stickers and ties. It has become the "in" thing to say. But what about practicing what we preach?

The philosopher Horace, who lived from 65 to 8 B.C., said "Seize the day, put no trust in the morrow." Wise words from a wise man.

His concern was that we put too much emphasis on the future and not enough on today. There are no guarantees beyond the moment. If all the great artists and authors of the world worried and waited until tomorrow, very little would have been accomplished. There are numerous examples but these are my favorites:

Goethe finished *Faust* at age 82.

The artist Titian painted *Battle of Lepants* when he was 98.

Michelangelo was almost 90 when he completed the Sistine Chapel.

Winston Churchill and Grandma Moses took up painting in their 80s.

Research shows us that nearly two-thirds of all great works in the world were done by people over 60 years of age. If they had worried about tomorrow, they never would have started. What a loss it would have been.

So forget time frames. If you have an idea that's worth doing, do it. Time was invented by man to serve him, not to enslave him.

Since life is but a journey, not a destination, it is wise to put up milestones along the way so you'll know how far you've come. Since we cannot mark the miles we have not yet traveled, we should not spend any time worrying about it. Better to have an overview of the plan and begin at the beginning. Concentrate on what makes you happy now, there may not be a future, but the present will be filled with good feelings and productivity.

That's what really counts when all is said and done.

Pessimism

Without reservation I can say pessimism is the ultimate ignorance. For many years my motto was "Always expect the worst and you'll never be disappointed." And I never was.

For a time I changed jobs faster than my underwear. Every time something good happened I managed to sabotage it. I walked around with what I call a "superior inferior complex" because mine was so much bigger than that of anyone I knew.

I actually reminded myself of the joke about two bums on a park bench. As a Rolls-Royce stops and a wealthy man looks at them, one of the bums says to the other: "There but for me go I!"

Slowly it dawned on me that my negativity was holding me back. To change the direction I was headed (which was down, down), I began reading self-help books, listened to tapes and went to seminars. Guess what? I found I enjoyed being me. I even liked being me. I'm okay, you're okay began to make sense. I stopped being hypercritical and super-judgmental and found myself being reproached less and less by my peers. My stress level dropped, pessimism gave way to optimism.

My new motto is "Always expect the best and you'll seldom be disappointed."

We have all that is needed to succeed in life if we can only discover the positive mental attitude that each of us has been endowed with. We must learn to transcend our self-imposed inner limits. If pessimism is the height of ignorance, then optimism must be the height of knowledge.

Trance-Formation

Transformation means to change one's character. We are all constantly changing—for better or worse. Just as our bodies gain and lose fat cells, our minds change direction, swaying this way and that, like the mighty Mississippi which can be raging downstream one day and be a dry sandbar the next.

So many of us are conditioned to think fatalistic thoughts. Chances are you are continuing to reinforce those negative energies. Despair, worry, hopelessness, frustration—are these common thoughts for you?

As far back as 1871, the scientist Charles Darwin recognized that "The highest possible stage in moral culture is when we recognize that we ought to control our thoughts." In his day, unlike ours, there were fewer distractions—no television, no arcades, no movies.

Today we are bombarded with data, much of it designed to gain control of our thinking and thus, our minds. Advertising is a form of hypnotism, hence my term "trance-formation."

Fortunately, the power to "untrance" ourselves remains ours. Unfortunately, unless we use it, we lose it. We must exercise the decision to remain in charge of what we allow as input. A helpful habit I have is to make believe I have a guard at the entrance of my mind who will either accept a new idea or dump it back outside.

Instead of sitting and being blasted by television ads for new and better cars, expensive insurance policies and a million things you don't need but think you must have, take the remote and turn it on "mute." A friend of mine does that and you would be amazed what grief she saves herself wishing for and desiring things she cannot afford. She uses the time to talk to her daughter and finds it amazing how much of a conversation she can have in the time it takes for a commercial.

By shutting out the temptations which put you in a negative mindset, end the "trance" that television fosters and "trance-form" yourself from a programmed robot back to a human being who can think for yourself.

"People are just about as happy as they make up their minds to be."

ABRAHAM LINCOLN

Where Are You Going?

Ever hear the old story told about Sir Thomas Huxley, the famous biologist and philosopher? He was on his way to give a lecture and hailed a horse-drawn taxi.

"Top speed," he said getting in. "Top speed, old man."

The carriage sped away. A few minutes later Sir Huxley asked the driver, "By the way, do you know where I'm going?"

"No, sir, your lordship," he replied. "But I'm getting there as fast as I can."

The story has a valid point: We rush through life but don't know where we're going.

Perhaps you have reached your goal in life and are now just jogging in place. If so, it's time to set a new set of goals consisting of both long and short-range plans.

A small winning minority of workers have developed a realistic set of Ps and Qs—P for purpose, passion and patience with Q for quality. It also stands for Personality Quotient which is just as, if not more important than, Intelligence Quotient.

Goal-setters understand that kites are safe when left at home but that is not what they are meant for. Kites were made to soar. It is the same with humans. Our goals should be kite-high yet reachable with good honest hard work.

So know where you are going, go as fast as your energy will allow, and get off the treadmill leading nowhere.

Procrastination

I was lecturing in the southeast portion of this country and kept hearing the phrases: "I'm fixin' to" and "I'm just about ready to."

These words are often used but rarely acted upon. Instead, they are used to push off something which needs to be done now, to an undetermined point in the future. When a pileup of things to do greets us in the morning, it makes it even more tempting to procrastinate.

I have a friend who bought a book about procrastination years ago and still has not opened it!

Procrastination makes us feel bad by keeping us on a treadmill going nowhere. It leads to a poor self-image. When used at work it leads to low productivity, which in turn leads to negative results.

To combat this insidious illness, I always recommend doing the most disliked task first so the rest of the day can be enjoyed. Instead, most people put off the most dreaded chore until the end of the day, thus insuring a bad day all around. Knowing you have an awful chore waiting for you puts you in a foul mood, which makes for poor communication with your co-workers. Everyone in the office, or at home, picks up on your negativity—in your body language and your voice.

To delay doing unhappy tasks will increase the time worrying about their completion, practically guaranteeing doing it poorly when the time finally comes (instead of doing it in the first place and being done with it).

Before going to bed each night I write down what must be accomplished the next day. The boring tasks go first so I get them over with. Then the day can end on a bright note rather than a somber one. If you make the first task your favorite, enthusiasm dwindles quickly after that and the list is never completed, or is completed in such a bad state of mind that nobody wants to be around you. When you arrive home at the end of a terrible day, your family bears the brunt of your foul mood. It's a lose-lose situation, all caused by procrastination.

These delaying techniques are a habit that can be broken in three weeks or less. Just begin at the beginning, don't eat dessert first, eat those hated veggies first, then enjoy the rest of the meal.

Problem-Project

Problem: a source of perplexity, distress or vexation.

Project: a planned undertaking.

Since "pro" means to move forward, let's take a look at these two words and what they can do for you.

A pro-blem moves you out of control when you are distressed or vexed.

A pro-ject puts you in the driver's seat controlling the ride.

A prominent psychiatrist who worked with thousands of patients found they were divided into two groups: those who lived in the past and thought "if only"—making them problem-oriented; and those who lived in the now and planned for "next time"—making them projectoriented. Obviously, the latter group coped more successfully with the ups and downs of life.

Generally speaking, pessimists are problem-oriented, negative thinkers and procrastinators. Optimists are project-oriented, positive thinkers and doers. For obvious reasons, optimists lead happier, healthier and more financially rewarding lives than their counterparts.

It takes the same amount of mental energy to think negatively or positively—to dwell on a problem or set up a new project. And the human mind has the unique ability to change itself (called a change of mind). All it takes is will power. If the tail side of a coin represents a problem and the head side a project, flip the coin in your mind and change the way you approach life.

Looking to the past for answers may lead to remembering old failures, while looking to the future leads to new thinking with positive goals in sight.

In my lectures I refer to our negative past as a garbage truck laden with trash. It moves very slowly because of the dead weight. If you dump the trash, the truck can speed up, taking you along on the road to personal success and happiness.

Remember that you are at the wheel. You can take the dead-end street called Problem or the Avenue to success called Project. Which direction do you want to take?

Pre-Game Strategy

It's that time of year again when America stops being a nation and becomes the arena of the world. I'm speaking about the clash of the Titans—the Super Bowl—the event that fills tons of newsprint, fuels Sunday sermons and makes gamblers out of the most conservative of men and women.

During the gladiatorial event, we can see what happened instantly and a slow-motion replay. We'll be told what occurred, why, and the dire consequences for the next few plays. During halftime, announcers will psychoanalyze the hows, whys and wherefores. They will drench us with their pearls of wisdom—as our thinking is done for us. All we have to do is grab a six-pack, a bag of chips and relax.

The advertising rates for this Day of Days are astronomical. The monies spent promoting products on Superbowl Sunday could sustain a third-world country for a year—or make a substantial dent in the national debt.

The idea of 100 million people watching two teams brutalize each other puts the savage old days of the gladiators to shame. They fought one-on-one, with other men or with lions. But in the ruthless game of football, giants (some weighing over 300 pounds) come charging from all directions intent on maiming or crushing their foes.

There's nothing else to watch for those of us who don't care much for this sport. I usually pass the day with a good book and pleasing music.

I guess this makes me somewhat unusual—in the macho sense, that is. I admit it. But I am not ashamed. Ralph Waldo Emerson wrote:

"Whosoever would be a man must first be a nonconformist."

I think he'd agree that it takes real guts for a guy to act for himself. So I'll take that as a sign that I'm a macho stud. Now if you'll excuse me, I have to turn off the Super Bowl and listen to the opera.

The Superbawl

No, that's not a misprint. This Sunday, millions of football fans will be foot-bawling because they lost zillions of dollars in bets on team and/or point spreads. As the football addiction reaches its annual climax, the suffering increases—women lose their husbands for the day, wallets are emptied and all constructive work is put on hold.

The majority of American males will spend the day watching the green area between the goalposts become a battlefield with dislocated shoulders, torn cartilage and bruised ribs. The cheerleaders will egg the teams on to "bash 'em," "crash 'em," "push 'em back, push 'em back, way back."

Four thousand years of religion has made us into vicarious brutes. We sit at home guzzling beer while enjoying the spectacle. Not only is this kind of violence accepted, it is glorified. On this day spirituality gives way to suffering; there is no serenity, only rough 'n tumble, hit 'em harder. There is no heaven, only give 'em hell and huge bonuses plus Super Bowl rings for the victors.

Call me un-American, call me pagan, but I'll pass on the guts and go for the glory of a quiet evening with no television, just my wife and me.

Amen.

"The real boundary in the United States is not the split between Democrats and Republicans, or between management and labor, or between whites and minority groups, or law-abiding citizens and rebels. The boundary is between 'fits' and 'non-fits.'"

FRITZ PERLS

The 10 Forgettables

Since most of our thoughts are based on worry, I'd like to submit a set of phrases that should be erased from our minds and vocabulary. They are as follows:

1. Court danger
2. Invite disaster
3. Entertain doubt
4. Expect the worst
5. Accept your fate
6. Hold a grudge
7. Wallow in pity
8. Drown in sorrow
9. Kill with kindness
10. Surrender to the inevitable

A good way to give up these bad habits is to understand worry. Psychologists have uncovered startling facts about anxiety which might be of interest since many of us spend up to 75 percent of our time agonizing over nothing.

Forty percent of worries never happen. Forty percent are already past. Twelve percent are needless concerns over our well-being. Most are petty, not worth even a moment's thought. A mere 8 percent is real, of which half—or 4 percent—is solvable!

This means that for every 25 worries you have, 24 are a waste of time, emotion and energy.

Think what would happen if you stopped this constant mental anguish and turned that time into productive channels.

Try a little test: Count the number of times you use one or more of the "forgettables" in a week. Then push your mental cancel button and reaffirm a positive solution instead. I think you'll find, as I did, that you'll soon forget your old worries and concentrate on what's good for you and your future.

Value-Added

I'd like to propose four E words to add value to everyday life.

Empathy, Encouragement, Enthusiasm and Excellence make human relations more humane when dealing with our peers, friends, immediate family, business associates, relatives and even strangers. It means, in essence, that we give something extra—above and beyond the call of duty, so to speak. In business the term is known as value-added.

If the research done by Stanford University in the eighties is correct, we only use 2 percent of our potential. When we reach the pearly gates of heaven, assuming we get there, St. Peter will ask us what we did with the other 98 percent of our potential. Are you ready with an answer?

As I have grown older and more mature, I realize that we can extend our aptitude through interaction with others. If you look through the history books, you will no doubt recognize that the "greats" of this world are known for achievements that benefit others (Pasteur, Madame Curie, Einstein—the list is endless).

One of my mentors, Johann Wolfgang von Goethe, wrote: "If we take people as they are, we make them worse. If we treat them as if they were what they ought to be, we help them to become what they are capable of being."

To that I'd like to add my own bit of philosophy on the subject of human relations: The more we give of ourselves, the more we have left over.

Selling Yourself

As the month draws to a close, take a moment to reflect on whether your values have become more positive. If not, here's a short sales pitch on selling yourself. It takes skill, imagination, fortitude and lots of courage. The results are well worth the efforts.

In my sales training seminars I use the following rhyme to enhance the spirit of the game.

Show and tell… Fail to sell
If you talk… They will balk
So instead… Use your head
Ask them why… And they'll buy

Most people love to discuss their favorite subject—themselves. By asking questions rather than making statements, you get them involved in the communication process. It works particularly well when selling a product or service. I recommend beginning an interview with a questionnaire to get to the root of the prospective buyer's problem. It shows you care. This attitude will open more opportunities than the conventional "barge-in-and-clobber-'em" approach indicated in the sales manuals.

If you want people to become interested in you and to buy what you are selling, first show an interest in them.

On job interviews, you'll find this technique is very successful. You can ask questions, too. It isn't a one-way street with you on the grilling end. Many prospective employers love to spout off about their company and if you are an interested listener, you get high marks.

Take this philosophy home. Try it with your spouse or significant other. Ask how their day went. Hold your own news for later. I think you will be amazed in the improvement in the interaction between you. Try it with your kids. They can bend your ear until it breaks, but I guarantee it will be worth your effort in the long run. Your kids will know they can talk to you. That's worth more than winning the lottery.

Here's a little exercise to get you started: Look in the mirror for five minutes and try selling yourself to you. It will take some practice but I know you can do it. I have faith in you. Have faith in yourself, too.

A Month for Expanding the Heart

Forgiveness

What better way to start the month than with a 21-day forgiveness diet? It works wonders on those of us who are truly ready to improve our lives. Too much valuable time is spent wallowing in anger, jealousy, resentment, envy and hatred—at both self and others. These habitforming, self-destructive feelings bloat us with negativity.

Here's the antidote: Make a list of all the people (especially family members) who you believe have hurt you in some way. Each day for the next three weeks you look at a name and in a normal voice say that you forgive them. This technique only works if you think and feel the words. Your own name must also be on that list.

By forgiving and accepting people the way they are, not as you would like them to be, the diet of forgiveness progresses and the bloating decreases. Forgiveness is a positive act which frees us from the chains that bind us to the past. To forgive is to give up the resentment and allow love to fill the space in our hearts.

Ditto for the self. Low self-esteem is resentment turned inward. If you stop being angry at you, love can enter your soul and only when you love yourself can you love others.

Do me a favor. Start today. Make that list and begin your diet. By the time we reach Valentine's Day you'll be two-thirds of the way through. You'll finish before this short month is over and I guarantee you'll feel renewed and energized. Trust me on this one.

Prescription for Life

Having given myself a doctorate in positive living, I would like to share a prescription for successful living. The formula is designed to cure "mental botulism"—a disease which affectsmuch of the adult population.

The prescription consists of Positive Vitamins or "Posimins" which are taken three times daily for 30 days.

Start with Vitamin A: Take one each of Attitude, Acceptance, Action and Aptitude. The aptitude pill will guarantee a positive outlook and will help your money-making skills. The action unit will get you going.

Vitamin B: Take one to Believe you are special and unique, capable of doing anything you really want. This unit will release much of your unused potential.

Vitamin C: Take one each of Caring, Confidence and Commitment. Watch how the caring pill helps you interact with others; look how the confidence pill makes you stand straighter and walk taller. Don't start the day without commitment to life.

Vitamin D: You'll need at least two of these, one for Desire and one of Dedication.

Vitamin E: One Enthusiasm pill will spice up your sex life. Need I say more?

Vitamin F: This will make you fearless, eager to face each day's challenges as opportunities for personal growth.

Vitamin G: Take two—one for Goals and one for God.

Vitamin H: Health and Habits are tightly interwoven. To eliminate bad habits take one dose of each per day.

Vitamin I: It is Important for your Imagination that two I units be included in the prescription for success—for yourself and for others. Everyone needs to feel important. It doesn't take any imagination to know that.

Vitamin J: The Joy of Living pill sums it up and completes this mega-vitamin-for-life prescription.

To find out if you need more or less of these vitamins, examine your attitudes and lifestyle.

"Those who cannot remember the past are condemned to repeat it."

GEORGE SANTAYANA

Patience

The ability to bear pain or trials calmly and without complaint is called patience.

I first learned the meaning of the word when I was 18 and fractured my left thigh bone. For three months I was bedridden, my leg raised and lowered by a series of ropes and weights. For an additional month I was wheelchair-bound, then I spent several weeks on crutches. Considering I had been on the track team and worked out regularly, it was pure hell.

Patience became my middle name. When I realized I'd be laid up for months, I gave in and opted for a new attitude. Without television or radio, I was left with the choice of staring at the ceiling or reading. I chose the latter and accepted my fate with optimism.

These days I need constant doses of patience as I travel from city to city on my lecture circuit. I spend hours in airports and hotels waiting. I need patience when my wife and I go out (she's always late) and a ton of patience for my 15-year-old son who already knows everything.

When you think about it, television is pretty amazing. Problems are solved in 30 minutes (20 if you don't count commercials). Life is not like that, which means that youngsters, like my son, are growing up thinking life's setbacks can be put right immediately. Wrong. They've got a lot to learn about patience.

How about you? Are you patient or do things like traffic jams and lines at the grocery store drive you nuts?

When you get impatient do you get testy and rude? Do you take it out on service people who are only trying to do their jobs?

All I can say is "chill out"—think about being flat on your back for three months—or longer. Waiting a few minutes in line isn't a big deal in the overall scheme of things. The world is not going to end, you are not missing an event of major proportions. Look around at other people, pick up a magazine, whistle a happy tune.

Relax and enjoy. Life passes by too quickly to get rattled over some small setback. Patience is a virtue.

Or, as Arnold Glasow says: "You get the chicken by hatching the egg—not by smashing it."

The Key

How would you like the key to positive living? It's really quite simple. Remember the old adage "Do unto others…"? Well here's a modern twist.

Do unto others before they do unto you. By that I mean, if you treat others better than they think they are, they will respond in kind to you and treat you better. The trick is to make the first move. If you greet people with respect, appreciation, admiration and gentleness, they will feel important. It's easier for them to reciprocate. In effect they will be "doing unto you" as they are now being done "unto." Makes sense, doesn't it?

I've recently read a book about a zookeeper who specialized in handling snakes with bad reputations. The bigger, tougher, meaner and more poisonous they were, the more she liked them. Some measured 25 feet! Using body language and words, she conveyed to the serpents that she respected them. They quickly responded by allowing her to pick them up.

The book also notes that rattlesnakes do not usually attack American Indians. From an early age, Indian children are taught to respect, not fear, snakes. The animal kingdom has great lessons for us if we care to learn.

You recall the Bible story of Daniel, who entered the den of lions and survived unmolested, and if you recall the stories of St. Francis of Assisi who communed with all sorts of animals through love, you'll see what I mean.

Use the key to positive thinking, use body language and an affirmative attitude when approaching all living things—human and otherwise.

Mirror, Mirror on the Wall

Wake up, brush your teeth, wash your face and look in the mirror. What do you see? A groggy face with hair that looks like an abandoned field of wheat. To change the image that stares back, you must work on the real you—not the man (or woman) in the mirror.

You begin the day only to find that your family, co-workers and friends don't listen to what you say. Some laugh behind your back, others ignore you completely. Their attitude irritates you. "Why can't I change them?" you might wonder.

I'll tell you why. You must change yourself first. That person in the mirror, that other you, that's who has to change before anyone will sit up and take notice. You want your hair to look like a well-tended wheat field but that takes work—and lots of it. To become the example of what you would like your peers to be, you have to understand that the only person who has control over you and what you become is *you*.

A Tip for Non-Tippers

For years I felt I was justified not leaving a tip when service was poor—or leaving only a penny so the server would know I didn't forget a tip but that I was making a statement. And what a negative statement that was. I thought I was being assertive, but all I was doing was setting up a losing situation with no lessons learned by either party.

Now that I have learned a little about life, I tip the standard 15 percent or more. I know that poor service isn't always the fault of the waiter—and that everyone goes through bad days. By leaving them a nice tip, I feel as though I may have turned a lousy day around for the better. Even if I don't, it makes *me* feel better.

Everyone has problems. The trick is not to burden others with them. That does not mean you should not seek advice from those you love and trust. Feedback is important. But it is also important to realize nobody can solve your problems but you.

Getting back to restaurants, I've also learned it helps to get your server's name. Instead of calling "Hey, you," or "Miss" or worst of all, whistling, if you can catch their attention with their name, you'll be delighted with the response.

Nobody in the service business likes to be treated like a dog or a slave. They are there to make a living and usually make less than minimum wage. Even though they are hired to wait on you, they are human beings and deserve to be treated in the same manner in which you would like to be treated. Remember the golden rule?

Mistreating others may give you a temporary rush of power but it only yanks you down and makes you feel foolish in the long run.

Take this little tip: In person-to-person situations, be as personable as possible.

In-Laws

In this month that celebrates love, I've got to deal with a thorny problem—my in-laws.

In-laws are not friends that you pick. They are thrust upon you by marriage. They can be quite the opposite of the sort of people you like to pal around with. They can have a completely different value system, political beliefs, even religious attitudes. Nevertheless, you're stuck with them and they're stuck with you. And, for the sake of peace, you must make an effort to get along.

My first experience with in-laws came when I was young and headstrong. They didn't buy into my lifestyle, nor did I buy into theirs. I thought they were "off the wall" to use an old sixties expression. When they tried to instill their traditions I resisted.

Over time, and with the help of what is called maturity, I found that I was at least half wrong when we didn't see eye-to-eye. And then—a miracle. I realized I was an in-law myself. Suddenly the tables were turned.

One day I discovered a wonderful acronym (you know I love acronyms). Ann Landers uses it all the time in her columns—MYOB, mind your own business. Guess what? It works.

Now, even though I am a professional speaker, I can sit for hours and listen. There were times when I nearly bit my tongue off wanting to interject my opinions. But I no longer have a need to force my convictions on anyone.

So the next time you're with your in-laws, try to remember that to them you're the in-law and act accordingly. The rewards of lowering your stress and blood pressure are greater than the victory of being right.

My previous in-law attitude is now out-lawed!

"If there is anything that we wish to change in the child, we should first examine it and see whether it is not something that could be better changed in us."

CARL JUNG

TLC

With so many mothers working outside the home these days, and nearly one-quarter of American children dropping out of school each year, it's becoming a major problem to treat kids with TLC—tender loving care.

Every day latchkey kids come home to an empty house. These little ones are forced at an early age to fend for themselves. Many of them are being raised by one parent. The extended family is quickly becoming a thing of the past. Grandmas and grandpas are not around to pick up the slack. The little victims of this era of new-fangled families become rebels with a cause—'cause nobody seems to care.

Old fashioned TLC required time at home, and quality time spent with the children. Since this is often impossible these days, I'd like to give a new spin on the old tune of TLC.

Trust them and let them know you care.
Love them and show them you do.
Competent, let them know they have the ability to succeed.

Giving these little tykes a sense of self-worth will help get them on the right road. Even if you can only spend a few minutes a day, let them know they are loved and that they are rich in spirit.

My father worked hard, he was rarely home, yet he instilled in my brother and me a strong ethical code. Talk less and do more, show your kids they deserve your TLC by positive reinforcement. Give them some small tasks and praise them when the job is done.

TLC comes in all shapes and sizes. There is no set pattern or amount. Five minutes of undivided attention with lots of praise is better than an hour of ho-hum activity. Pick the TLC package that best suits you and use it well. Cherish what it can do for the future of your precious family.

Options from Within

Opportunity once knocked on a man's door but he didn't answer because he was too busy looking for a four-leaf clover in his backyard.

Ideas and opportunities come out of nowhere, when we least expect them. You've got to learn to listen with a "third ear."

Most people go through life in neutral with little trust in their innate potential. If the man searching for a four-leaf clover had listened to what opportunity was offering, would he have taken a chance? Or would he have hesitated, thinking he didn't have the fortitude to do the job?

If you were to define a plan for life, shored up by a strong sense of purpose, there would be no limit to your untapped potential.

The first step to developing a sense of purpose is to know yourself. The second step is to change yourself based on what you discover is the real you, what you want out of life and what your long-term goals are. This is easier said than done. Nevertheless, persistence will bring permanent results.

The third step is hardest of all—do not try to change others. Make and set goals for yourself, attain them and become a shining example. Let others do the same for themselves. Trying to alter the personality or set goals for others is a fruitless and anxiety-provoking chore that can only lead to frustration and bad feelings.

Concentrate on you—what you can do to make your world a better place in which to live and thrive.

Loving Yourself

Why do we pick on our faults and magnify them into personal calamities?

We stand in front of the mirror and whine: "I'm ugly," "I hate my wrinkles," "I have terrible skin," "My thighs are fat."

Suppose you said those things to your best friend. Do you think you'd be friends for long? Would they put up with that verbal garbage? I don't think so. Yet you think it is all right for you to say that to yourself. Well, it isn't.

It is masochistic to behave like that. The only way to present a positive image to others is to love yourself—warts, fat thighs, bad skin, wrinkles and all. With negative affirmations you risk becoming what you think you are since the mind does not act as its own filter.

When the bad seeds you plant in your psyche grow to maturity, you're in trouble. So doesn't it make sense to plant the seeds of love instead of hate?

If I stress affirmations it's not because I have become a broken record. I stress them because they are the only way off the treadmill many of us mistake for the road of life. Think positively and you will become a positive person. If you think negatively, you drain your mental and emotional reservoir and will become an empty shell that must draw from others to exist. Who wants to be around someone like that? They are toxic people, they take your good feelings and substitute their bad ones.

So celebrate Valentine's Day by standing in front of that mirror and thinking good thoughts about yourself. That's the order of the day. You can have the weekend to work on it before I come back on Monday to motivate you again.

Learn to love those wrinkles, those thighs, those flaws. Everyone has them. Nobody is perfect—at least nobody here on Earth. But a word of warning: Don't go searching out other people's flaws to make yourself feel better. Learn to accept yourself as you are and you will naturally accept the flaws in others.

Happy Valentine's Day. Love yourself first.

Front to Back

There is a magnificent statue of Buddha in a Chinese temple. As the story goes, the Emperor asked the sculptor why he was spending so much time making the back of the statue as ornate as the front when nobody would see it. "The Buddha will see it," was his humble reply.

How is your back? Are you putting up a good front? What persona do you present—what facade do you show?

During the day I wake up a man and quickly become a husband, father, customer, friend, employee, confidant. At night I am a speaker and an author. During any given 24-hour period I can have nine different personas.

The question is, do I show my whole self to all those I interact with, or do I just show my front side and hide my back? Do I show myself wholly or just partially?

Think about some of the common expressions: to stab someone in the back, to talk behind someone's back, to turn one's back. Those all have negative overtones. People like to keep their back against the wall so they are not vulnerable.

However, if I only give the front side, I am holding myself back—literally. When I socialize with others I must use my whole self, not just half. Only by using all of me can I really reach out and touch others in a positive and productive way.

So if your back's up against the wall and you are only presenting half of yourself to the world, take a giant step away from the wall and let others know that you are a whole person, with a front and a back.

Others may be tempted to use your vulnerability against you. However, a positive attitude will help deter them. And what is the worst that can happen? They'll talk behind your back, say bad things. So what? Names will never hurt you. By transcending their pettiness you make yourself a better person. You rise above them, as well as your old past.

On Listening

Friendships are easy to cultivate if you talk about *them,* not you.

One evening my wife and I ran into some acquaintances. When I noted the foreign accent of the woman who accompanied them, I asked about her country of origin. We quickly launched into a discussion of Peru. Although she did most of the talking, I'm sure she'll remember me warmly.

I am a speaker by profession yet I make it a point to listen to others. People are drawn like magnets to good listeners since there are not many of us. Even those who seem to be listening often suffer from a malady known as "listening with a deaf ear." They nod and smile but really don't hear what you are saying.

The friendly listener understands that tone is often more important than the words. Words lie, inflection conveys emotion. A person can say "Everything is fine," but an astute listener will hear the underlying message that "Everything is a mess."

Tune into tone, which leads to emotion, which leads to sympathetic listening. Listen because you really care and are honestly interested. There's nothing worse than spilling your guts to someone who is not the least bit concerned with your problem. They nod and smile like a Kewpie doll. It can be very discouraging and painful.

Listening is a form of loving. There's far too little of it going around these days. So make it a point to spend some time every day paying close attention to your spouse or significant other, your children, parents, friends and co-workers. It takes away from your own time but I can practically guarantee that when you need a sympathetic ear, you'll find one easily if you've been a sympathetic ear yourself.

"Faults are thick where love is thin."

JAMES HOWELL

*"If we had not faults we should not take so much
pleasure in noting those of others."*

LA ROCHEFOUCAULD

Puppy Love

My mother was brought up in a strict orthodox Jewish home in Czechoslovakia. She was taught that all animals were "untouchable" except for ritual slaughter. When I bought my first puppy, a Chinese pug, she recoiled in horror thinking the dog was a large ugly rat.

Frisky was the most lovable creature I had ever met. She earned her name and was the epitome of unconditional love. If only I had learned what she had to teach me when I was younger, I could have saved myself a lot of grief.

To her credit, Frisky won her way into my mother's heart. In fact, she was the first animal my mother ever touched—because she was touched.

Mom came from that old-fashioned school that says love and affection are not openly displayed. Although my dad did not demonstrate his love, my brother and I knew we had a special place in his heart. In fact, the first time he ever told me "I love you" was when I confided in him about my impending divorce at age 39.

Frisky had no such problems showing her love. Without a care in the world, she'd snuggle right up to people—even strangers. She had a joie de vivre that was truly a marvel.

We can learn much from animals like Frisky—loving creatures who have no fear and no hangups—who love unconditionally with no ifs, ands or buts.

If only humans could be more like their pets!

ESP

By now you know I love acronyms. While most people will read ESP as Extra Sensory Perception, it also stands for Exaggerated Self-Pity. I see this pitiful state everywhere and hear about it more times than I care to repeat.

It invariably begins with: I, me, my and is quickly followed by ulcers, in-laws, boss, problem and progresses to poor me, pity me, nobody loves me.

Once we take possession of a problem by calling it mine, we are stuck—as though we'd used mental crazy glue—and become a victim.

There is a way out of this trap. To truly understand we must go back to ESP—the original extra-sensory perception.

We are all endowed with an innate perception. This includes insight, intuition, inspiration and imagination. If we are made in God's image, then imagination is God in action.

By shifting our mental emphasis, we can change our way of thinking and become a winner instead of a whiner.

Take the letters ESP and decide how you want to use them. Just to make the situation even more confusing I'll add one more possibility: Extra Special Person.

The choice is yours. As for me, I'll skip the Exaggerated Self-Pity and use my Extra Sensory Perception to make me into an Extra Special Person. How about you?

Dress Rehearsal

We are all familiar with dress rehearsals—the practice sessions before weddings, plays, etc. Everyone "dresses up" as though the performance were real to gauge the potential for success. It also serves to get rid of last-minute glitches and thus guarantees a happy occasion.

To carry this notion one step further, I suggest we use mental dress rehearsals or affirmations—power-driven phrases—to help us practice for life's unexpected glitches.

The key to making these affirmations work is to feel and visualize the positive results that will occur. Then the mental dress rehearsals become real since they are governed by your mind.

Negative affirmations also work—but in the reverse. You get what you feel you deserve if you imagine it strongly enough. The result will be ongoing unhappiness. The choice, once again, is yours. Planting weeds and expecting flowers to bloom is unrealistic. So, too, planting negative thoughts will not yield positive results.

Choose the ideas you want to govern your life. Rehearse them in your mind. Let them become part of you and give you strength.

Let's say you have a meeting with your boss. Play it over in your mind. How will you approach it? If you know he will be finding fault with your work, practice how you can turn his negativity into creativity without becoming defensive. Imagine what areas he will concentrate on and you will know, through mental rehearsals, the best way to make him look right without making you look wrong.

Let's say you come home from a hard day's work and your wife says: "We've got to talk." Dread. Gloom. You've done something wrong. She's going to lower the boom... maybe.

Before the "discussion" takes place, mentally prepare yourself to be neutral, to not pick an argument or become defensive. A sensible way to approach the situation is to listen to her side then say you need some time to think about it. During your thinking time, mentally rehearse how you will counter what she had to say.

Mental dress rehearsals go a long way toward calming rough waters and making sure life goes more smoothly.

The New Commandments

If you stop and think about it, the 10 Commandments are pretty negative. Their message is valid but it is always in the *not* mode. To counteract this way of thinking, I have come up with a new set of six positive commandments that should bring out the best in us.

Commandment One: You will love yourself unconditionally—even if you have fat thighs, a triple chin, pimples and warts. You will accept the fact that you are made in God's image and God does not make mistakes.

Commandment Two: You will respect all living things beginning with you. This will include family, friends, peers, co-workers and strangers. You will respect animals, flowers, plants and insects, knowing they are part of the ecological scheme of things.

Commandment Three: You will praise, appreciate and recognize others whenever possible. Our deepest hunger is to feel important. This is a very effective, cost-free method of motivating people you come into contact with. You will find them ready to reciprocate and you'll get much more accomplished than you ever believed possible.

Commandment Four: You will give your time and money to those less fortunate than you. It's a sure-fire stress reliever when you shift your concern away from your own problems to those of others.

Commandment Five: You will live in the now—the present. It is the only time frame you have any control over. The past is over, the future has not yet come. The present is your "present" from God. Use it wisely, do not squander it, enjoy every moment, work honestly to make it better.

Commandment Six: You shall pay careful heed to the foregoing commandments for they can guarantee you peace of mind and spirit and make this a positive instead of a negative world in which to live and raise your children.

Manners

Does anybody teach children manners these days? Or are people so manner-less that they can't?

I spend a good deal of time traveling and I am a keen observer of human interaction (or lack of it). Not long ago I was in Nashville, Tennessee for a seminar and two incidents that happened almost simultaneously really got me thinking about manners.

A husband and wife were having breakfast in the hotel restaurant. They were nicely dressed and I would have assumed they had good breeding, but the husband sat there smoking and reading the daily paper, completely ignoring his spouse. She sat opposite him, sipping her coffee, bored to death. When she lit a cigarette I imagined her setting fire to the newspaper and would not have blamed her for doing so.

A few tables away two men were having an animated discussion, waving their arms and hands. The waitress did a juggling act just to avoid spilling the contents of the breakfast tray. I marveled at her dexterity but groaned at the lack of sensitivity of those jerks.

Two examples back-to-back of men ignoring women. The two men took the waitress for granted, with not even an acknowledgment that she was bringing them their food. The husband pretending the wife was not even present is a sad commentary on life and manners in general. Can you imagine her doing that to him? He'd have a stroke.

I was not born a doormat; neither were you. We only become doormats if we allow others to step on us. Assert yourself when it is appropriate. Let others know you count, you are a person, you deserve respect. Show others your good manners and hope that they follow suit.

Manners are learned early on and follow us through life. If you are a parent, please make sure you teach your offspring well. If you are already grown and feel your manners could use some improving, go to the library or bookstore and get a book on manners. It is never too late to learn new tricks. Don't wind up like those rude men in the hotel restaurant.

"Every individual has a place to fill in the world and is important in some respect whether he chooses to be so or not."

NATHANIEL HAWTHORNE

The Ties That Bind

In my closet are two sets of ties—one for my livelihood and one for my social life. Today I wore an atrocious tie to a business appointment. I did it on purpose so I would blend in.

There I was in my ugly tie trying to sell myself, but it was not just my tie doing the talking. The tie was the price of admission which gave me the opportunity to practice what I preach.

Here are some tips that I have found beneficial when interacting with others.

- Deal with people on an emotional level. Success is determined by attitudes, not aptitudes. Using factual information alone will not sway people toward your ideas. You must motivate by stirring their emotions.
- Try to be a people person. Several years ago a survey of self-made millionaires showed one common denominator—they saw the basic good in people. They were builders rather than critics.
- Follow the Golden Rule. Look at the world through the eyes of others and do unto them… humane relations work best.
- Cultivate the art of being dependable. People will pay more attention and more money if you exhibit dependability—a rare commodity these days.

Show and Tell

Gaining the confidence of strangers is amazingly easy. I call it Show and Tell, like the game we played in first grade.

People, in general, enjoy sharing—from recipes to deep dark family secrets. I'm sure some therapists would be green with envy if they knew that I could learn in minutes what it has taken them years to squeeze out of their clients.

I believe confession to strangers is a cheap form of therapy that provides a catharsis to purify ailing souls. Unfortunately, while it relieves the teller, it burdens the listener. A new set of problems has been hoisted onto a set of previously innocent shoulders.

When approached by strangers who want to spill their guts, I try to stay on light topics by talking about the weather, current events, hair styles or their children. Good vibes tend to keep conversations off the darker side.

And if by chance you do get an earful of someone else's bitter lot in life, try not to make those problems your own. They will work it out their own way. You are simply the vehicle for lightening the load, so to speak. Shrug off bad vibes by thinking positive thoughts.

If you find that your favorite hangout is crowded with negative energy generated by the clientele, maybe you should consider changing hangouts. There are plenty of places to shop or get a good bagel these days.

The Change Quotient

Most of us are afraid of changing—ideas, jobs, significant others (even if they are abusive). We are prone to leaving things as they are, no matter how illogical or painful.

For years I watched my previous wife cool her cup of soup with an ice cube while I have waited patiently (and impatiently) for mine to cool naturally. One day, in a rush, I decided to try my wife's trick and popped an ice cube into the hot broth. Surprise. It worked. When I think of all the times I have burned my mouth over the past 10 years, I could kick myself for being so stubborn.

How is your Change Quotient? Do you resist like a mule or are you simply a slow changer like me?

They say our body cells replace themselves every 11 months, giving us a completely new physical body every seven years. If only our thinking could change at that pace. Imagine having a new lifestyle every seven years. It would keep us from aging since we would spend much of our time getting ready for the new stage of our personal growth.

Unfortunately, most people are set in their ways and would not even consider changing, not even a bit.

Since the ice cube caper I have realized there is hope for me. Perhaps I need to step up the pace and not wait 10 years for each little victory over my ego.

How about you? Are you willing to try something new? Perhaps once a week is not too much to ask.

Try a new restaurant; watch a new program on television; take a walk going on a different route; talk to someone in your office you've never spoken to before; if you have a beard, shave it; if you are smooth skinned, grow a moustache; if you read fiction try a biography; taste a new food; buy yourself something you've never worn before. It's easy, really, to add a new and different spice to your life.

Remember, nothing ventured, nothing gained.

P.S. Kudos to my ex-wife for never saying "Jacques, I told you so."

*March
Yourself into
Positive
Energy*

Goldfish

If you have goldfish and want to be entertained, take them out of their bowl and put them in the bathtub. Amazingly, they will continue to swim in a small circular pattern, rather than using the full length of the tub. Before you keel over laughing, look in the bathroom mirror and ask yourself why you don't take full advantage of your potential. I can assure you, your powers of reasoning are far greater than those of goldfish.

We use only a fraction of our capability, which means we have plenty of room for expansion.

The goldfish hits the glass sides of his small container when he tries to swim further. So, too, we hit the glass walls in our mind—those negatives that tell us we can't go any further, we can't do it better, we are not bright or competent enough.

Those walls were erected in our childhood by thoughtless words spoken by people who loved us. Most of the time they meant well, nevertheless, our interpretation of those careless words is what makes us who and what we are.

Have you ever told your child he or she was an idiot or called them stupid—even in jest? Those cruel words are internalized and made a part of their personality. Have you called them slobs or dummies or clumsy? If so, you are adding to the negativity that will follow them throughout their lives. You can stop making those comments and help your children become positive adults.

As for your own built-in bad feelings and thoughts you must stop accepting the wrong messages given to you by co-workers, bosses, spouses and even so-called friends. You must learn to replace them with a new way of thinking.

Eleanor Roosevelt once said: "No one can make you feel inferior without your permission."

If you do not give permission, your self-esteem will grow. We are all created in God's image. Yet it is up to each of us to maintain that image no matter what harmful words and thoughts are thrust upon us.

Change comes from within. Don't be a goldfish swimming in circles.

All the News Unfit to Print

On a daily basis the newspapers are filled with garbage—stories about the low-lifes that inhabit our planet and wreak havoc on the lives of others, destroying their property and taking innocent lives.

I, for one, have decided to exercise my right of freedom of the press by not reading these types of articles. I'd rather focus my attention on the good things, not the evil ones.

It seems that there is an unspoken taboo on treating others with tenderness. Yet to grow as a human being, it is necessary to "reach out and touch someone" at every given opportunity. We can "touch" someone with words and ideas, not necessarily by physical contact.

During my lectures, when I reveal tidbits about my personal life, I touch my audiences with my sincerity, which in turn earns their trust. Once the trust is established and they are listening, I can deliver my message to an attentive group knowing they will weigh my words carefully.

There is good news everywhere if you look for it. Upbeat stories abound, sandwiched in between the bold headlines of mayhem and murder. Stay focused on the moral issues, try not to get sidetracked by the madness. I guarantee it will keep you in a healthier state of mind and, thus, a healthier body as well.

"You get the best out of people when you give the best of yourself."

HARVEY FIRESTONE

Bloom Where You're Planted

Two thousand years ago the Egyptians buried a clay vessel containing wheat grains. When archaeologists discovered and planted the seeds, they were amazed to find the grain had retained its full potency as they began sprouting within days.

My question is this: If 2,000-year-old grains can retain their full potency for growth, what is the full human potential for personal development?

If we have nearly 100 billion brain cells interconnected into infinite possibilities, why would we want to go through life cursing our lot? Why would we want to die without ever touching the greatness that lies within each of us?

Just as the wheat grains retained their power for growth, we, too, maintain a reserve for personal growth. If we only use 2 percent of our potential, then we have 98 percent waiting to be developed.

Let's say that you earn $40,000 a year. If you unleash your untapped potential by only 1 percent, you increase your earning power by $20,000. How did I figure that? If you only use 2 percent and can earn $40,000, then one-half of the 2 percent is $20,000. By increasing your potential output, you can increase your annual salary to $60,000. The sky is the limit.

Some Mary Kay salespeople once complained to me that it was difficult keeping up a high performance schedule and they found themselves pulling back before resuming their hectic pace. I explained that when they reached new highs, they are leaving their "comfort" zone, which threatened their self-esteem. While they felt good making better sales, they wondered if they could keep up the pace under pressure which led to a temporary slump.

The answer is yes, you can do it. With a high degree of self-esteem you can break sales records right and left. You can set new industry highs and you can keep it up if you don't let self-doubt creep in.

We all have the same potential as the 2,000-year-old wheat seeds. Bloom where you're planted.

The Ultimate Oxymoron

There is a book called *Obsessive Love*. As far as I can determine, this is the ultimate oxymoron. For the uninitiated, an oxymoron is a contradiction in terms—like jumbo shrimp.

Obsession is defined as an unnatural longing: "a persistent disturbing preoccupation with an often unreasonable idea or feeling."

Can we call that love? I doubt it. Love should not be a disturbing or unreasonable feeling. Love is positive; it should not be negative.

People who want to change others lack self-love. By manipulating someone else, they take the pressure off themselves to change from within. All their energy is focused on controlling another being. It is hard work to change oneself, it's much easier to bully and bash someone else into behavior modification. That is not love.

When someone new comes into our lives, the first thing we usually do is start turning the dials, as though they were a washing machine being tested for the rinse, wash and spin cycles. We want them to conform to our way of doing things. When we make unreasonable demands we strip them of the personality that first attracted us to them.

For many the *idea* of being in love is the turn-on. They don't love the person, per se, they like the idea of controlling someone else.

I believe that love is the greatest proof of our aliveness, but only if we are allowed to operate as distinctive beings within the relationship. If I stop being me and start being what my wife wants me to be, that is not love. If my wife were to beat me or become obsessed with me that would not be anything that could remotely be called love.

If someone asked me if I loved my wife even though she did those terrible things to me, and I answered "yes," I hope that person would cart me off to a therapist to find out why I had so little self-esteem that I would allow someone to treat me in such an abusive way.

Love can only grow in a nurturing environment. Anyone reading this who says they are in love and are floundering in a negative place with their spouse or partner, should turn off the television and take a good hard look at the reality of their world. Then do something positive. Don't be an (oxy) moron.

Combat or Comfort?

Following up on the previous thoughts, let me ask whether you are going through life in a combat or a comfort zone.

The "terrible twos" are our first real combat zone as we try to match our new-found independence against parental restraints. As we grow into adults, most of us find a niche in life that we find comfortable. It doesn't matter if it's in a nine-to-five job, or being a homemaker, or being a corporate executive jet-setting around the world.

There are ups and downs to living in whatever cookie-cutter style of life we have adapted. The ups are that we feel comfortable and we earn a nice living. The down side is that it stifles imagination and creativity. It limits the potential we have for making life a richer and more adventuresome place.

We all want to live in a comfort zone, where life goes smoothly and day-to-day stress and strains are kept to a minimum. When we find ourselves in a combat zone, we try to escape as quickly as possible.

Perhaps there is a happy medium—like a comfort zone from which we make calculated trips into the combat zone, just to see how we can use it to our advantage.

Instead of accepting things the way they are, we should expect them to change as we learn to create new horizons and set new goals for personal achievement.

Another Oxymoron

I like oxymorons as much as I like acronyms. This one is Constructive Criticism.

Constructive implies a positive position, while criticism implies a negative outlook. The very nature of the inherent ambivalence of the term destroys the credibility of anyone to professes to use it to solve any type of personal or business problem.

Constructive criticism is also self-destructive if used on a regular basis as self-criticism. It borders on mental and emotional suicide if done habitually and shows a low self-image at work. We get enough censure from others, why heap more on ourselves? And don't you just love it when constructive criticism is done for "your own good"?

If you want to do something for my own good, make it good—not bad. I have already internalized so much old mental garbage from my childhood I don't have room for more. I imagine we're all in the same boat. Any form of criticism reinforces pessimism, making it more difficult to respond positively.

The good news is that anything we have learned can be unlearned by using newer and stronger attitudes to replace the outdated ones. You can turn things around by allowing only positive images to flow in, while filtering out negative images.

Beginning and ending your day with positive affirmations is like framing your awake time with health-giving bookends. You will sleep better if you use constructive wisdom.

Problems

Who doesn't have some problems? Raise your hands. I don't see any hands going up. Okay, we all have problems, some are life-threatening and Earth-shattering. Some are of virtually no significance in terms of living and breathing. But even the tiniest obstacle can be a nettle that festers.

So I have devised some basic rules to keep you mentally fit, emotionally balanced. They will also keep you from becoming a royal pain to those close to you.

Rule #1: Don't complain. Every time you do you reinforce the problem giving it more power over your life.

Rule #2: Avoid complainers. They are toxic. They cripple you mentally with their negativity.

It will be hard to follow these two simple rules. We all love to complain, which in turn means we must listen to others complain. But it keeps us on a negative path. So instead of whining and moaning, try to see a positive solution to your dilemma and try to encourage your friends, peers and family to do the same.

"A good problem statement often includes: (a) what is known, (b) what is unknown, and (c) what is sought."

EDWARD HODNETT

"A problem well stated is a problem half solved."

CHARLES F. KETTERING

Sex

My eyebrows shot up when I heard my 13-year-old son telling a classmate he had reached his sexual peak. For once I was truly speechless. Since that astounding conversation, he has learned that a man's sexual peak is at 18. So he has something to look forward to.

Call me a prude, but I worry when 13-year-olds already feel they know all about sex. When you stop and think of the overt sexual references and explicit scenes contained in movies, videos, television and even commercials, it boggles the mind. Why mess with the unstable egos of teens? They have enough confusion about their identities without making boys feel they have to be macho studs and young ladies feel they have to look like hookers.

I long for the old-fashioned days when youngsters were in no special hurry to grow up. We did things when it was time. Nowadays I see 10-year-old girls with makeup so thick they look freakish. They are trying to appear older. They smoke to act "cool." But they are failing miserably. True maturity involves the ability to make intelligent decisions based on our own self-worth, not what others think we should be.

Parents have a hard time when their offspring prematurely decide to be adults—or at least act the way they think adults act.

I have spent, and will continue to spend, many hours explaining to my son that he has to be true to himself and not Calvin Klein. It's a lonely battle we wage as parents. There are times when my point is made, and times when it falls on deaf ears.

I can only pray that he learns to feel good about himself as an adult. I'm keeping my fingers crossed—that's about all parents can do aside from locking their kids in closets until they turn 21.

Rent-a-Life

A few years ago I addressed a convention of a company that rents everything. After my keynote speech, I spent the rest of the day strolling through the Miami Beach Convention Center looking at the rental exhibits.

Imagine spending your whole life never buying, only renting. From coffee pots to cars to apartments, you need never own anything. The only thing missing was a booth called Rent-a-Friend.

How many of us are lonely? Loneliness is a state of mind, not a physical problem.

The trick to getting through life in a rich and rewarding way is not to need people but to like being with them. If we need outside stimuli to feel good about ourselves then the rent-a-friend idea will be just the ticket. If, however, you can turn inward and become your own best friend, you will never be bored or alone. Since like attracts like, you will soon be surrounded by people who want to be in your good company.

Perhaps Rent-a-friend is an idea whose time has come. It is this kind of forward thinking that made the company that rents everything a success.

Why Clone That Clone?

It's been said that until age 20 we continually worry about what others think of us. That concern tapers off gradually until we reach 40. By then we no longer care. And by age 60, we discover that most people never thought anything about us in the first place! What a lot of wasted worry and anxiety over nothing.

Teens tend to dress just like the friends they hang around with. The preppies, the jocks, the dweebs, the skinheads all have their own dress codes. The only thing I notice once I get past the clothing is that none of the groups initiates original thinking. Thus, they fail to use the one constant which they inherited at birth—their innate intelligence. Clones following clones reinforce the old adage that misery loves company.

In this high-tech world only a minority of those destined for greatness use their brains for something better than a hat rack. Less than 5 percent of all workers become movers and shakers. The ones that do are the creative thinkers who choose not to follow the herd.

Uniqueness is within each of us. Not to make the best use of this positive quality means remaining average—in other words dull. Today's kids may be smarter with their mastery of computer technology, but that does not make them wiser. When it comes to common sense it is practically nonexistent.

Facts, figures and friends form the bulk of the collection amassed during the high school years. Ethics, values and skills for dealing with interpersonal relations are left behind in a dust heap.

Two centuries ago, the writer Charles Caleb Colton said "Imitation is the best form of flattery." That may have been true when there were role models who had integrity, honesty and commitment to bettering themselves.

More recently Ralph Waldo Emerson said "Imitation is suicide." By that he means that copying others kills our own spiritual uniqueness.

By adding one more quote from the English poet Samuel Johnson who said "No man (woman) ever yet became great by imitation," we can see that you must *be yourself.*

Bagels

One morning I went to a bagel emporium in the mall. There was nobody else sitting near me so I assumed I had the server's complete and undivided attention when I gave my order.

"Two eggs over medium, one well-done poppy bagel, light on the butter, and coffee," I said in a clear crisp tone.

The server jotted down my order and repeated it back to me to make sure there were no mistakes.

"Two eggs over easy, sesame bagel lightly toasted and heavy on the butter." At least she got the coffee part right.

As I waited for the order to arrive, I pondered the lack of communication that is so prevalent these days. Perhaps the server had some heavy-duty problem on her mind, perhaps she was wondering what to make for dinner or what time she had to pick up the kids from school.

Too often we are involved in "psychobabble" when we should be paying attention to what others are saying. This inner noise shuts out all incoming information putting us at a disadvantage if and when we need to repeat it back—as in the above illustration.

The American Management Association indicates that communication is the most important part of any one-on-one situation. The sender gives a message, the receiver picks it up and digests the material. Both must agree on the information transmitted.

Unfortunately for me, the server that morning had other things on her mind.

Listening is a form of respect. The Golden Rule applies here: Listen to others the way you would like to be listened to."

If I were behind the counter taking the breakfast order, I hope I would have had the courtesy to give the customer my undivided attention when he or she was speaking. Once the order was given to the kitchen I could return to my own inner talk, at least until the next customer was ready to order.

The next time you order in a restaurant, it might be a good idea to have the server repeat your order. Otherwise, don't be surprised at what is put on your plate.

How to Succeed at Business

Let's take a closer look at the word B-U-S-I-N-E-S-S. Note that the U comes before the I. Personal development comes first when it comes to handling people.

If we go back to past role models, an interesting pattern emerges.

Marshall Field, department store magnate, said: "I simply practiced honest, slow-growing business methods and tried to back them with energy and a good system."

Sir Thomas Lipton, tea mogul, said: "I was careful of the slightest detail and took care that my customers always went away pleased."

In other words, instead of trying to manipulate the client, they concentrated on their own personal skills and traits. These days manipulation is the buzzword—getting others to conform to our wishes. Is it a wonder that we often fail to get the desired results? Then we blame others for being too ignorant or too stupid to appreciate what we have to offer.

The secret of success lies in developing your own talents and abilities to the max. Strive to build personal integrity. Honesty stands out like a sore thumb in the marketplace these days.

"There is nothing so powerful as truth," said Daniel Webster. "And often nothing so strange."

Today the business person must dig deep into his or her belief system and put it on the table so to speak. We are all looking for trust—a value which cannot be compromised.

Remember the movie, *How to Succeed in Business Without Really Trying*? Well, I'd say there is no such thing. Trying is the key to success—trying to improve your own personal values and then trying to convey them to others so they can see what you have to offer, not only in the way of product, but also in integrity.

That is the real key to success.

"Success is a journey, not a destination."

BEN SWEETLAND

"Six essential qualities that are the key to success: sincerity, personal integrity, humility, courtesy, wisdom, charity."

DR. WILLIAM MENNINGER

Fall and Win

An old axiom says that in order to win you must fall many times. This is seen dramatically in toddlers learning to walk as well as ice skaters competing for gold medals. Every time they fall (fail) something is learned. Eventually failure turns to success.

The trick to using failure as a springboard to success is to keep your eye on the ultimate goal. Since the fall immediately becomes the past once you hit the ground, use the goal to pull you up again.

It is no different in the business world. The end result must remain stronger than the pitfalls encountered along the way.

Fall and Win only works if you learn from your failures and not repeat them over and over again. In my seminars I find many people who are literally afraid to falter and, therefore, don't take chances. These terrified people cannot possibly succeed—their own fears hold them back.

In the end it's not how many times one falls but how quickly recovery is made. Haven't you seen ice skaters who flip and slide across the ice, pick themselves up and continue without missing a beat? That kind of swift unbroken recovery counts at scoring time.

Learn to take the lumps and bumps of life in stride. Try not to get shaken by the negatives that tumble your way and knock you down. Each shakeup can lead to better and bigger business accomplishments. Just as failure feeds on itself, so does success.

Think about the wise words of Alfred Lord Tennyson in his poem "The Day Dream":

> *This proverb flashes through his head,*
> *The many fail, the one succeeds.*
> *Make sure you are the one who succeeds!*

No "Ifs"

The Chinese language is written in symbols that are most intriguing. They do not use individual letters like we do.

For example, when they combine the symbols for man and woman, it becomes the word "good." If only life were that simple. If only we could learn to treat our partners with unconditional love. The problem as I see it is that there are too many prerequisites in any relationship.

Too many people treat love on an "if" basis. In the New Testament we are asked to love our neighbor. Note that it does not say "if."

Generally speaking, and there are exceptions, neighbors will be neighbors we love, admire or dislike in the same proportion that we love, admire or dislike ourselves. We project our own insecurities to the outside world.

Rodney Dangerfield made a fortune with his phrase "I don't get no respect." Respect from others comes back to you only after you are able to appreciate yourself.

You are a good person, able to help others, able to give when needed and listen when others have problems. Then why not treat yourself with the same unconditional love you would give to someone else who had all the qualities you admire?

Good feelings start at home. Home is where the heart is. So open your heart to your own love—whether you are a man or a woman, and be good to yourself.

Death Row Woman

A woman wrote to Dear Abby and signed off with these chilling words: "Death is better than surgery. I'm damned if I do and I'm damned if I don't."

She was referring to breast cancer and the surgery needed to relieve her symptoms. While I find her story touching I cannot fathom how death would ever be preferable to an operation. Disfigurement is not something anyone can accept easily, but dying is not the answer.

To destroy a vehicle because it is flawed would be like tossing a car because the stereo is broken or a tire is flat. Cosmetic disorders do not require such drastic measures.

The medical evidence continues to mount that a majority of illness has its roots in unresolved emotional conflict. Bottling up raw emotion can eat away at us—literally—causing cancer, ulcers, migraines, tremors and nervous twitches. Losing control over one's life is the beginning of these self-induced diseases.

Many of us heading into the 21st Century are programmed to self-destruct because we believe we are not cosmetically acceptable. Again, I repeat, these notions come from the home at an early age. This is known as the Quasimodo Complex.

Parents must develop positive images for their children. Good looks do not count for everything. Look at the woman who is "damned" because she will be physically imperfect after the surgery. For her, life is no longer worth living. A sad statement indeed.

Breaking 100

People are living longer. According to the United States Census Bureau there may be one million centenarians by the year 2080. What I find interesting are the often contradictory reasons given for their longevity.

The University of Kentucky pried the secrets from 546 centenarians. Here are some of the things they credited:

- An ongoing loving relationship with a spouse or child.
- An upbeat outlook on life.
- Helping others.
- Never taking medicine.
- Drinking Scotch!
- Creating good will in their environment.

To me it looks like love works, positive thinking works, and helping others works.

Some of the participants were obese, some were recovering from cancer. Yet at age 100, they were still alive showing that their hearts are in the right place.

Living a century, from the days before indoor plumbing and penicillin, to the days of men on the moon and Valium, is amazing. It is a great tribute to mankind's endurance.

On a day-to-day basis, we should look at the quality of our life if we want to reach the century mark. Life is frustrating, there are immense sorrows each of us will experience. We will have ups and downs, peaks and valleys—an emotional rollercoaster ride. Enthusiasm, love, good will and a positive outlook will benefit us in the long run.

As for not taking any medicine and drinking Scotch, I cannot say for certain. I only know that just as inner turmoil can lead to debilitating diseases, living an upbeat lifestyle will prolong the inevitable and give you a rich and rewarding time here on Earth.

Space

When my family lived in Brussels, Belgium, all four of us lived in two rooms—a bedroom and a kitchen. Talk about needing my own space. The bedroom had two beds, one for my parents and one for me and my brother. That didn't leave much room for anything else. The bathroom was in the hallway on an upstairs floor.

When we moved to Casablanca as refugees, we lived for three years in one tiny room on the Rue de Tunisie. Before we were given that extravagance, the French put all displaced persons in horse stables. We slept in the stalls!

In 1943 we came to America and rented an apartment on Houston Street in Manhattan that was positively huge by our meager standards. It had two rooms plus a half-kitchen. My brother and I slept on a foldout couch in the living room. What luxury.

In time we moved again to a three-room flat in the Williamsburg section of Brooklyn. We were coming up in the world.

When I joined the Air Force I shared sleeping quarters with three other airmen. Once again I was a "no-space" cadet. Upon my discharge I found a small room with a foldaway bed at the 92nd Street YMCA. I called it home but it wasn't much bigger than a closet. At age 25 I had privacy at last, even though I had to share a bathroom down the hall with 50 other souls like me.

My next step was to share an apartment on East 91st Street. My roommate was a singer/composer and a steady stream of musicians and artists came and went at all hours of the day and night. That's how I met my first wife.

We moved in together in an apartment across the street from Central Park. From the 19th floor we could see the park and the east side of Manhattan. It was a dream come true.

Many years later, as I sit in my office in my home overlooking Long Island Sound, I can breathe at last. It has been a slow steady climb but I have arrived. And let that be a lesson.

In the immortal words of Walt Whitman: "Every cubic inch of space is a miracle."

"Beauty is only skin deep, and the world is full of thin-skinned people."

RICHARD ARMOUR

"As I grow to understand less and less, I learn to live it more and more."

JULES RENARD

The Brain

The best description of the brain I have run across is: "a universal receiving station attached to a limitless bio-computer." Then why do we use so little of it?

Suppose your car had a 100-horsepower engine and you only used 2 percent. You'd be crawling down the highway at a measly two miles per hour!

We can put higher octane in the gas tank, or eat high energy foods but that won't help much. We can push our foot down on the accelerator or push our bodies to do more. That helps a bit. But the real clincher is to rid our minds of the negative energy that holds them back.

If we cannot get rid of the negatives, then we must use a positive force to attain constructive growth.

Look at the great pitcher Nolan Ryan. He is 44. By baseball standards he is over the hill. Yet he recently pitched his seventh no-hitter. His mind has not accepted his physical limitations, allowing him to compete with men half his age.

Watch the tennis greats like Jimmy Connors on the senior tennis tour. While he doesn't pit himself against today's tennis superstars, he can still smash the heck out of a tennis ball. His legs may not be young but his spirit is.

Accepting our physical limitations and letting them hold us back is like trading in a car just because it has reached a certain mileage. If the vehicle gets you where you are going, why not let it do its job? So, too, as long as you can get up in the morning and get your mind and body functioning, give it your all. See if you can get your car and your mind to add one additional percent so you can go three miles an hour instead of two.

Try not to let those negatives "I can't do it," "I'm too old for this," creep in. Stay positive and focused on your goal. That's using your brain.

Reunion

Recently I attended my 40th high school reunion. The class of 1951 of Eastern District High School met and reminisced.

After graduation I entered the Air Force for a four-year stint. I had lost touch with my classmates and I expected them to look as they did four decades ago. Surprise!

Some had white hair, others had none. The ladies were mature with age lines on their faces but their eyes still sparkled. Some were grandmothers.

I spotted my first girlfriend and my closest buddy. There was enough hugging and kissing to last another 10 years.

As I surveyed the room I realized that my physical and mental age nowhere approximates my chronological age. I still have that childlike eagerness for life. I wondered how many of my former classmates have kept their zest for living at the same level it was back then.

Growing older does not have to bog us down. It will slow us naturally and gradually. But there are people who see a wrinkle and feel ancient, or experience an ache and pain and give up their favorite sport. Get over it! Wrinkles are a sign of maturity. Do some stretching exercises to get through the aches and take your favorite game a little slower.

As for me, I can't wait for my 50th reunion. I hope to be spry as a spring chicken—in mind, spirit and body.

Symphony of Life

Music is food for the mind. The music you listen to parallels the role vitamins play in keeping you sound and healthy. My favorites are the classics, written by composers whose lives were touched with genius.

There is an analogy here and it goes like this: You are the conductor of the symphony of life. Attach a musical section—strings, brass, percussion and woodwinds—and you make each performance unforgettable. Synchronize the four sections so they play in perfect harmony. The result is satisfying every time.

The strings deliver the lightest sound, or the spiritual side. The brass, with their earthy tones, represent the physical. Percussion with its steady beat parallels your mental development. And finally, woodwinds with their wavering timbre, imitate the ups and downs of your career. A careful blend of the four important areas governing your daily activities will help you live in a more stress-free environment.

We are all given sheet music for life at birth. It's what we do with the score that counts. Some never play the tunes and die without every hearing the music within themselves.

Putting your musical act together takes creativity and time. Symphonies are not written overnight. You must take life one note at a time, trying to hear the theme in the music you are creating. Some parts will be intense, other sections will be slow and lingering, still others will be dancing tunes.

The movie *Mr. Holland's Opus* is a wonderful example of how a man put the symphony of his life together—working on his lifelong dream of a musical masterpiece. He managed to find the time to compose even though he was distracted by the emergencies of life—a deaf son, the demands of his job, students who needed his attention and a wife who stayed by his side even when he was too busy for her.

Yet above it all, Mr. Holland stayed true to his goal and, at the end of the movie, we are all touched by his dream coming true.

While your life may never be captured on film, it is just as dramatic in its own way.

Orchestrate yourself well, listen to the music within.

Fear of Success

Talk to people about success and failure and you'll get some strange looks. These terms are opposites. While many people fear failure, they don't understand the concept of fear of success.

In working with a group of financial consultants in a seminar on Goal-Setting and Success, I was struck by one word which appeared again and again—guilt.

These executives wanted to know how to get rid of this psychological mental block which affected their lives in such a negative way. We explored where its power came from and how they carried it from the past into the present.

We found out that guilt was laid on them by parents, teachers, friends, peers, siblings, bosses and religious leaders. Anyone wanting control over someone else merely has to press the guilt button.

To get rid of the fear of success, we must let go of those guilt feelings that are buried in our psyches.

Getting your act together as an intelligent, mature person begins with uprooting the guilt from the deep recesses of the mind. Once the guilt is gone others will lose their control over you. They can push the guilt button all they want but nothing will happen.

Guilt is a waste of time. It accomplishes nothing. What's past is past; nothing can change it. We judge ourselves too harshly on what is gone and should be forgotten. How many of us would give a million dollars to take back a hurtful comment or a wrong deed? We can't change the past. It's over and should be forgotten.

We possess the power to look forward, not back. Don't drag the past into the present and cloud a perfectly beautiful future.

Bumper Stickers

Bumper stickers say a lot about the people around us. This past week I saw the following ones. I have substituted the word "love" for the heart symbol.

I love my German Shepherd, I love my cat, I love my ferret, I love my parrot.

What I have never seen is: I love my wife, I love my mother, I love my husband, I love my children.

Why do we advertise love for animals and not for human beings? Are we ashamed to admit love for anyone except a pet?

I'm not ashamed. I love my wife. I love my son. When was the last time you said to your spouse or child "I love you"? If you haven't done it in a long while they will probably think you've lost your marbles when you do say it.

We profess our love and undying devotion at funerals—when the deceased can no longer hear us. What a waste. The time to say sentimental things is when the living can hear us and respond.

Parents, tell your kids you love them. Read the obituaries for a few days and you will see the importance of this.

Children, tell your parents you love them, *now*, while they are still alive.

Ladies and gents, tell your spouse or significant other how you feel, honestly and with emotion, not "love ya." Say it with feeling, in a quiet place. Life is too short to do otherwise.

"In music one must think with the heart and feel with the brain."

GEORGE SZELL

"Love doesn't make the world go 'round. Love is what makes the ride worthwhile."

FRANKLIN P. JONES

*Living for
Your Dreams*

April Fool

On this day of practical and nonsensical jokes, many of us make fools of others—and ourselves. That's nothing new for me since I've always considered myself a nonconformist and have often been called a fool by those who are unenlightened.

The great philosopher Henry David Thoreau said, "If a man does not keep pace with his companions, perhaps it is because he hears a different drummer. Let him step to the music which he hears, however measured or far away."

Thoreau wanted each man and woman to follow his or her individuality and not be herded around by the crowd.

For years I have tried to follow this philosophy and it has not always gone well. I lost a job because of a beard I wore as a young man; I lost a chance at a promotion because I would not wear a necktie. I have always objected to being controlled; I prefer *guidance*. Instead of conforming I left the company even though I was a top producer, and signed on with another firm that saw beyond the need for a necktie.

When I was younger, my mother called me a rebel; my dad said I was a revolutionist. They thought I'd end up in the electric chair—and I did. I bought an electric Barcalounger when I moved into my Manhattan apartment. Thank goodness they didn't knock the "crazies" out of me or my life would be dull and mediocre.

We have the power to think for ourselves yet we allow others—parents, teachers, employers, and anyone in a position of authority—to think for us. We let them dictate what will make us happy.

What delights me has nothing to do with what delights you. Some people are happy at nine-to-five jobs, others cannot stand the thought of working set hours. Some women want children, others shudder at the thought. Some people like to work with their hands, while still others cannot do any manual work happily.

Conformity suits some, nonconformity suits me to a tee. Each to his or her own I say.

Flaunt Your MBA

Here we go with the acronyms again. My MBA is not a college degree, but a diploma from the school of hard knocks. It stands for Magnificent Being in Action.

Too many of us go through life without being self-actualized. In other words, we don't find any meaning or fulfillment—our lives are poor in spirit, not rich as they were meant to be.

Abraham Maslow, a psychologist who lived from 1908 to 1970, wrote: "A musician must make music, an artist must paint, a poet must write if he is to be ultimately at peace with himself."

Is there a musician or artist hiding inside you? If the answer is yes, what are you doing about it? If you are repressing a strong desire to create because you don't have the time, or ambition or money for supplies, you will never know the joy of realizing your full potential.

Climb out of the rut you're standing in. Move ahead without so much as a glance backward. Go and follow your *feelings* (for once do not listen to what the mind tells you). Who knows, it may unlock an enthusiasm you didn't even know you had. You can be *you* and not who others think you should be.

Self-actualized people don't wait for someone else to push the elevator button. They use the steps by doing instead of waiting. They fully understand that the universe is always in a state of creation.

MBAs make things happen. Like the old story about the two frogs.

Two frogs fell into a vat of milk. One decided he could not swim. He sank to the bottom and drowned. The other—the one with the MBA—began to swim at a furious pace. The milk turned to butter and he climbed out of the vat easily.

When you run into difficulty, do you become a turnaround or a churnaround?

Time

The old and the new: a clash in time.

One day a Calculator Clock (CC) was put next to a beautiful wise old Antique Clock (AC). CC began babbling at breakneck speed; AC tried to slow it down. If we could overhear them, their conversation would sound like this:

CC: How old are you?
AC: I lost count after the first hundred years.
CC: How fast does your clock beat?
AC: Twice per second.
CC: Wow! That means you beat 120 times per minute.
AC: I guess so, I never tried to figure it out.
CC: Figuring things is easy for me, I'm programmed. If you beat 120 times a minute, that's 7,200 times per hour. That's a lot of beats.
AC: Think so?
CC: Do I ever. Let's see, that's 172,800 beats per day. You sure are busy.
AC: It seems that way.
CC: Holy cow! You beat 63,072,000 times per year.
AC: Those are big numbers.
CC: And if you're 100 years old, we multiply by 63 million… oh no, I can't… the numbers are running off my screen.
AC: Slow down kid. Just add two zeroes to the 63 million and you have 6.3 billion.
CC: How is it possible to beat 6.3 billion times without having a nervous breakdown?
AC: I never looked at how many times my pendulum swung. I only concentrate on the next beat. That makes the tick-tock go nice and steady.

Are you like the CC, always getting ahead of yourself? Live in the now—not the past or the future. The present requires your full attention. Today is the best day of the rest of your life.

Are Goals Enough?

Let's take a close look at eight prominent and successful men who met in one of Chicago's most prestigious hotels in 1929.

Five were presidents of huge corporations, including the New York Stock Exchange and the Bank of International Settlements. One was a member of the U.S. Senate, one was a speculator on Wall Street and the last was the chairman of the world's most powerful monopoly.

It is safe to assume that these giants of the corporate world reached their goals in life. They were fabulously successful, rich beyond their wildest dreams and powerful.

As their achievements grew, they replaced their original values for more power. Families were abandoned and love for people was transferred to things. Their all-consuming greed for more spelled disaster in the end. Their fall was certainly more swift than their long, hard climb to the top.

One died bankrupt, one was a penniless fugitive from the law, one went insane, two served time in prison, and three committed suicide.

I hope the lesson has not been missed. History repeats itself if the conditions are right. I believe any goals we set should be more than just financial. Interpersonal relations, affection for others and charitable acts cannot be abandoned for material wealth. Money ebbs and flows, like the tides.

Goals are great in soccer, but I really believe the game should be played for its own sake.

Happiness

Happiness does not come in a slam-bam explosion. It comes in bits and pieces, sneaking up on us when we least expect it.

You can have the radio on and only after music has been playing for a while do you realize that it's your favorite composition. Your mood changes and now you find yourself delighted.

The good news is that we can do this at will. We don't have to wait for the disc jockey to put on our preferred selection. To put it another way, we can choose to be happy any time we want. All it takes is a mental decision.

For an experiment try telling some bad news while smiling. It is virtually impossible since smiling changes negative thinking to positive. I have tried this again and again and find that nobody can tell bad news while grinning.

As William James said: "In order to become enthusiastic, you must act enthusiastically." Act happily and your mind will come up with reasons for being happy. Beats negative thinking any day.

The greatest happiness comes from doing for others. It is also accepting yourself as you are.

So as the popular song goes: "Don't worry… be happy."

"I would I could stand on a busy corner, hat in hand, and beg people to throw me all their wasted hours."

BERNARD BERENSON

"Happiness? That's nothing more than health and a poor memory."

ALBERT SCHWEITZER

Peace

Peace is defined as freedom from civil disturbance; a state of security; freedom from disquieting or oppressive thoughts or emotions; a pact to end hostilities.

In other words, peace is the absence of a negative condition. This word does not stand alone as a positive quality, but rather as an opposite condition to something bad.

Peace of mind is achieved when we rid ourselves of negatives. This can be time-consuming and expensive (when we add up the cost of therapists, psychologists and psychiatrists).

In fact, spending years in therapy reviewing the negative side of one's life tends to reinforce pessimistic attitudes, hence, for many, there is no cure for living in the past.

If I understand the concepts of peace of mind correctly, I believe it encompasses the notion of loving oneself. Think of words like tranquil, calm, relaxed, meditative, harmonious, at one with the universe. Those are the nuggets of peace of mind.

Tranquility can override the bad times. Norman Cousins, who beat a life-threatening illness, says that the will to live is very strong if we feel loved and are loving. It can throw doom and gloom out the window if we decide life is worth living and enjoying.

Blueprints for Life

You're buying a new home and you've just seen the blueprints. The property has a superb view and you are excited at the prospect of things getting started. Problem is, your builder goes over the blueprints day after day and nothing is accomplished.

If this sounds familiar—if you procrastinate doing what needs to be done—I have a life plan for you. There are six "rooms" in my blueprint: the physical, mental, spiritual, financial, social and family life rooms.

Each of my rooms has a goal and no "buts" are allowed. Buts are the stumbling blocks that epitomize low self-esteem. We put them in front of our daily sprint so we cannot get started at all.

Action must follow plans. It comes naturally to those who are not paralyzed by negativity.

Getting rid of the cranial crap should be our first concern. Instead of running from room to room and doing nothing, it is better to pick one aspect and start down the road to developing that area—whether it is financial, a better family life, or mental and physical wellness.

I know a woman who was falling apart physically at age 56. She had poor muscle tone, shortness of breath and a tumor. For years she did nothing to improve herself. Then, one morning, she awoke and realized the end would be premature if she didn't get going. She hired a personal trainer, went on a strict diet which included herbs and vitamins. She began eating healthier and working out every day. Within weeks, her eyes were sparkling and her spirit had improved. The doctor was amazed to find the tumor shrinking.

Draw out your blueprint for life, then get into action. Don't sit there in a catatonic state. Get moving! Get motivated!

Start building the rest of your life into a monument *now!*

Cleanup Time

If we all take responsibility for our own cleanliness, the world will be a nicer smelling place in which to live. When we clean our minds, or, as Voltaire said "Cultivate your own garden," we benefit ourselves and, likewise, make this world a more optimistic place in which to live.

Did you know Co-op City in the Bronx was built over an old dump site? The builders did not unearth the old garbage, they covered it up with high-rise housing. On the surface, it looked like they turned lemons into lemonade.

But there is a down side to the story. Many of the 55,000 people who moved in brought their old negative mentality. Or did they pick up the rotten vibes that lay below the basement?

Outside improvements are meaningless unless the inside is tidy. Would you move into a house or apartment without cleaning and painting first? I think not.

So, too, with our minds. We must get rid of the old garbage and replace it, not cover it up. Push out the old before instilling a new and more constructive way of thinking.

Self-improvement begins at home and spreads to all facets of our lives. Clean your mental house of old detrimental ways of doing things—procrastination, sloppiness, disinterest—and replace them with functional and practical topics.

As the poet Pablo Neruda says: "All paths lead to the same goal: to convey to others what we are."

Accept What You Expect

"People grow old and die because they see other people grow old and die," said the Hindu philosopher Shankara.

Expecting the worst is the route of least persistence. Notice I did not say the path of least resistance.

Conversely, expecting the best can be the way to increase our enjoyment of life. Why can't we all live to be 100, like George Burns and Irving Berlin? If you plan to live a century, don't you think that you'd stand a better chance than if you only plan to live to age 50?

Think young and the body stays young without suffering the ravages associated with the aging process. Think old and the human machinery breaks down since you accept what you expect.

I know of a woman who stopped having birthdays at age 33. She tells everyone she meets she is 33 although she has a daughter who is 24! No, she was not a child bride. But people believe she is much younger than she actually is because she doesn't feel her age and doesn't act it.

If you want to lead a timeless life, try not complaining for 21 days. Not only will you save a lot of wasted words, people will react very favorably toward you.

As Bennett Cerf so wittily put it: "Middle age is when your old classmates are so gray and wrinkled and bald they don't recognize you."

You don't have to be like your old classmates. Think young and you'll feel the same.

Endowments

Years ago I worked with a major insurance company which sold retirement, or endowment, policies which were redeemable at age 65. It astounded me how many people put their trust in the sales reps who sold these often useless policies, instead of putting trust in themselves.

Investing in one's own personal development can never depreciate in value and will bring enormous dividends over time. Investing in right ideas and thinking will make you more precious. It will give you a healthy outlook unhampered by worry about the future.

What do you invest your time in? Do you input useless and negative information? Or do you stay on the positive track, finding practical projects to do and reading good literature instead of trash?

When was the last time you took a course to better yourself? A woman on welfare wrote to a nationally syndicated advice columnist that she was having trouble getting a job because she wasn't suited to anything advertised in the paper. Instead of whining about how she cannot do anything useful, that woman should sign up for a typing course. If she lived in an area where being bilingual is helpful, she could pick up a Berlitz tape and learn another language. In other words, make productive use of your time. Invest in yourself.

If your job involves a great deal of writing and you are unsure of your abilities, don't hold yourself back. Sign up today for a writing course. Become a skilled wordsmith, then look to the next level up in your company and set your sights on it.

Women often find themselves in dead-end positions. They think they can become executive assistants, but rarely executives. There is no reason why they cannot take management courses and move up.

Instead of buying insurance policies that may or may not pay off when you die, invest in yourself. Make your own endowments to YOU. They will make you truly rich.

"Let everyone sweep in front of his own door and the whole world will be clean."

GOETHE

"Middle age is when your age starts to show around your middle."

BOB HOPE

Pancakes

For eight years, my previous wife made pancakes for me on Sundays. It was a treat I looked forward to with relish. Then suddenly one morning my wife greeted me with the following declaration:

"If it wasn't for those darned pancakes you insist upon having every Sunday, I could get my work done earlier and enjoy the day."

"I thought you liked pancakes," I replied, surprised and hurt.

"I hate them," was her reply.

The lesson? Communication, or rather a lack of it.

Why did it take her eight years to let me know how she felt? And why didn't I read her body signals? After all, that's what I teach—communication.

Fortunately, my wife met me halfway. She agreed to make pancakes for my birthday, July Fourth (which declared her independence from the chore), Labor Day (reminding me of the work involved), Thanksgiving (we all gave thanks for the delicious tasty treats smothered with butter and syrup), Christmas and New Year's Day—a perfect six-pack of pancake days.

If you suspect a problem with interaction, either at home or at work, watch body language more closely. I am always lecturing that God gave us two eyes and two ears, but only one mouth. This means we should see and hear four times as much as we speak.

Keep the information lines open and flowing both ways. In this case my wife never should have allowed such a long time to pass before telling me how she felt. Similarly, I should have been more tuned in to her early morning rumblings. Any relationship is a two-way street. Try not to barrel headlong down the road thinking nothing is coming from the opposite direction. You may be in for the crash of your life.

Going Bust

Call this the hardware bust caper—a true story that I saw on television.

There was a modest hardware store in a small town, located right next door to a Christian bookstore. The hardware store was going under, ready to declare bankruptcy, when the owner had a bright idea. Since most of his customers were men he figured he would give them an added attraction when they came to shop.

So he dressed two of his shapely female clerks in nothing but a G-string and a smile. Instead of the store going bust, the busts are keeping the store going.

I have always admired Yankee ingenuity, but using nudity to sell tools—or sexploiting workers—degrades women and demeans those involved, buyer and seller alike.

There is a time and a place for everything and I believe nudity in a hardware shop is not one of them. What happens when a man brings his young son or daughter? Kids just aren't ready for that kind of thing, even if Pop is.

It would be interesting to note if business would continue to expand if the only exit from the store were through the Christian bookstore. That might put a moralistic damper on things.

I personally think that making money at the expense of women is indecent and immoral.

Licenses

This may or may not be a true story, depending upon your point of view, but the moral is quite clear.

There was a man on line at city hall. Behind him was a couple, very much in love. The first was waiting for a license for his dog. The pair wanted a marriage license. The clerk, in a world of his own, had the first man fill out a marriage certificate and the couple, who had other things on their mind, inadvertently filled out a dog license form.

And so it turned out that the dog license is until "death do us part," and the marriage license is renewable every year.

Come to think about it, that makes more sense than ever before with 50 percent of all marriages ending in divorce. Consider the reduction in attorneys' fees if this were the case, and the emotional damage that could be spared. Wedding guests could give a check dated a year in advance. If the blissful couple makes it to their first anniversary, they can cash it.

The story about the license may be my fable, but the lesson it teaches should be learned well by anyone considering marriage or longterm attachment.

Make sure it is for real. Think about where you will be in a year, five years, 10. Is this the person you really want to spend time with or are you just bored, lonely or wanting to start a family?

Get married for the right (positive) reasons, not the wrong (negative) ones.

40th Anniversary

Speaking of marriage, let me say congratulations to my previous in-laws who have recently celebrated 40 years of wedded bliss.

The festivities took place at a beautiful rustic inn where the food and ambiance were superb. Except for a few minor glitches, the affair went splendidly.

There was a humorous moment when one of the guests sang a solo rendition of the anniversary song in a tempo none of us could follow. That event was quickly followed by the matriarch of the family exclaiming in a loud clear voice that she hated the raisins which were found in the apple strudel.

Oh, if life could be so simple.

If people could spend nearly half a century together with such minor problems, there would be more marriages staying together instead of falling apart. But this is not the case.

All too often, small things are blown completely out of proportion by one party or the other, and a major catastrophe ensues. Add drinking and a bout of fisticuffs, and disaster is the result.

As we approach the new century we should all make a concentrated effort to maintain the sanctity of marriage with our partner instead of looking for the fastest and easiest escape route.

I, for one, am looking forward to my 40th anniversary. I'm on my way and going strong. How about you?

In Defense of Fruitcake

I have to share this astounding piece of information with you. The Pentagon is sinking in the paperwork that governs its 134,000 employees. Along with over 30,000 pages of regulations and more than 4,000 laws, it has 20 pages on fruitcake and seven pages on pencils.

Perhaps that is the reason screwdrivers cost $700 each—$3 for the tool and $697 for the paperwork!

AT&T's old operating manual devoted over a thousand pages to addressing the issue of taking orders.

We are drowning in verbosity, there is a plethora of wordiness. Where is Abe Lincoln when we need him? He used 266 words to move the nation. The 10 Commandments, the rules which have governed many of the world's religions for centuries, were written on two tablets.

The government, a hotbed of red tape, threatens national productivity by overwhelming us with endless details, forcing us to look downward rather than outward.

Empowering people with more responsibility seems to motivate far better than the fear of breaking company policy. Trust is the buzzword of employers toward employees. New chances for greater achievement and the possibility of higher wages produce optimum creativity in the workplace.

People want to feel significant, they want to know they are making a difference—to see tangible results from their effort. Most workers will give more than 100 percent of themselves if they know they have a sense of purpose appreciated by the company.

Employers must break old habits of holding workers in check to gain the most from their productivity. Keep rules and regulations to a minimum to get the maximum from the work force.

As for the Pentagon and the conglomerates with their tons of paper, I can only surmise that the fruitcakes are in charge.

"The critical period in matrimony is breakfast time."

A. P. HERBERT

"The great secret of a successful marriage is to treat all disasters as incidents and none of the incidents as disasters."

HAROLD NICHOLSON

Artificial Intelligence

For centuries we have been using what may be called Artificial Intelligence (AI). Perhaps that is why the world is in turmoil. AI incorporates some of the most convoluted thinking imaginable.

A famous Yankee baseball manager once said: "If people don't wanna come to the stadium, how are you gonna stop 'em?"

I'm still puzzling over that.

How about the British bus company that allowed half-empty vehicles to pass lines of passengers waiting at bus stops. The "intelligent" excuse?

"We can't stop for passengers because it would interfere with our route schedules." What?

If the proper use of mental energy is intelligence, or the skilled use of reason, let's not get sidetracked by artificial intelligence which makes no sense.

Thinking a project through, trying to visualize all the pitfalls and drawbacks, takes common sense and genuine intelligence. In our haste to get where we are going, too many of us get sidetracked—like the bus driver who didn't have time to pick up his passengers.

Attaining your goal is just a matter of putting one step in front of the other and progressing in a logical fashion to the end.

As Anatole France put it: "If 50 million people say a foolish thing, it is still a foolish thing."

POM Button

My favorite button is not on an article of clothing. Instead it sits on my television remote and is labeled "mute." When I mute the incessant blaring of commercials, I weed out what I truly want and need from what society dictates I should have.

The POM button gives me Peace of Mind, hence the acronym. By destroying the unwanted noise pollution, I give myself the freedom to choose based on my personal requirements.

In order to feel good about yourself, you must make decisions about what you will allow as input—as well as output.

Those car commercials are tempting—sleek, shiny new vehicles taking corners without spilling a cup of coffee, or with champagne glasses stacked upon the hood and not shaking. The bottom line is that your car probably gets you where you are going for a lot less per month. When you shut these people and their endless babble off, you suddenly realize you don't need what they are selling at all.

Another happy button for me is the one that erases unwanted recorded sales messages on my answering machine. More seductive words that try to entice me away from my hard-earned money.

Now if only we could weed out the negatives that surround us by pushing an invisible button that made *toxic people* mute.

Apathy

Ask people if they are for or against apathy and chances are they will say they don't know. That's a rather apathetic answer right there.

Not long ago I gave a free lecture at the New York State Secondary School Student Association (NYSSSSA) on maintaining a positive attitude.

Of the 75 schools invited, only seven sent representatives. I guess they were suffering from TA (Terminal Apathy). Too bad, they missed a wonderful opportunity to interact with their peers and hear a great lecture—no modesty here.

The ones who came were terrific. After my talk on personal motivation, they stayed for an extra hour asking intelligent questions. I guess if 10 percent of any group can get excited about their life and future, all is not lost. They will be the ones to move mountains in the future and maintain America as a world leader.

These kids will not be like the Dick Dullards of the world, never taking chances, making only the smallest demands on life and never reaching full potential. Like a watch without hands, Dick's mind died years ago but his body keeps on ticking—going nowhere fast.

The young adults who came to my lecture will be more like quartz crystal watches, vibrating steadily as they strive for their goals.

Even the Dick Dullards of the world can change—if they want to. Age is no barrier when a great idea arrives. Ben Franklin was a prolific inventor, working well into his eighties. He firmly believed that there are no rules to success that will work—unless you do.

Remember, the world does not owe us a living. It will continue to run long after we are gone. It is far better to have tried something and failed than to have tried nothing and succeeded.

At least I can rest in peace knowing there are some bright young men and women out there ready to make good things happen.

WEATHER

Weather is a universal topic—used with strangers, and even at intimate parties, to keep conversation at a safe level.

The times are few and far between when people are pleased with what Mother Nature gives us. They complain constantly: too rainy, too dry, too hot, too cold, too snowy, not enough snow (for skiing), too windy, too still—you get the idea.

Long ago I learned to accept the weather as is and not fret about it. My schedule adapts, my plans can be modified. It beats fighting it mentally and physically. And I try to avoid the complainers—they can turn a sunny day cloudy or a rainy day into a miserable experience.

To make a dismal day bright, surround yourself with pleasant people, those who see rain as a necessary ingredient to green grass or a good excuse to see a movie.

To put it simply: Make the best of it and quit your whining!

Jackdaws

The jackdaw is a small, Eurasian black and gray crow who focuses on bright shiny objects and snatches them up. A jackdaw learns his collecting at an early age from his parents and never gives up.

Children also learn at an early age—accumulating shiny and valuable bits of information which they internalize. Their unique ability to color the world is soon disciplined and reorganized by those who "know better." (Or should I say should know better?)

First there is surveillance—monitoring what goes into their delicate system. Next is evaluation that chips away at a child's self-esteem. Next is the reward system which pits one student against another instead of making them more cohesive. Finally competition is introduced which extinguishes the last creative spark.

Is it any wonder that kids are rebelling at school and at home? They feel betrayed by the system, judged by unqualified adults whose job it is to ignite and develop the creative spark.

Parents and teachers should not use fear or reward, but allow attitude motivation to rule the nest.

What does this have to do with jackdaws?

Allow children to decorate their internal nests with all the bright shiny objects they can find. Let them sort through the possibilities without censure, promise of reward or fear of failure. The more experiences a child can put in the hopper, the smarter and more creative he will become as an adult.

"It is easier to be wise for others than for ourselves."

LA ROCHEFOUCAULD

"Yesterday is a cancelled check; tomorrow is a promissory note; today is the only cash you have—so spend it wisely."

KAY LYONS

Snails and Peaches

For the happiest 12 days of my life, I must return to 1940.

My family was living in Brussels, Belgium, and on May 10th the Nazis began bombing the city. We watched and waited anxiously as they prepared to invade. Meanwhile, my father went to the town hall to pick up our passports so we could leave.

We left four days later and headed to the south of France where I was to spend the best time of my young life. That's where I discovered snails and snakes and ate peaches and cherries in the cleanest, freshest country air I ever smelled.

The snails came out after spring showers and slithered along the roads leaving glittering trails. The snakes were the small garden variety and didn't bother anyone but they fascinated my brother and me.

The peaches were enormous and juicy. My mouth is watering now as I write about them. We would pick them off the trees. And the cherries were the best I've ever tasted.

There were cows everywhere, calm, serene, laden with milk. We drank it fresh with no homogenization or pasteurization.

In retrospect I admit that one of the reasons everything tasted so good was the newness of it all. Since those carefree days in Villaries, fruits and vegetables have been saturated with pesticides, milk is processed, nothing is fresh any more.

I don't make it a practice to live in the past, but it's always nice to recall a few happy scraps from my younger years. I miss the tranquility and slower pace of less industrialized countries. I don't find that speed means better accomplishment. The opposite may be true. Speed often means sacrificing aesthetics.

Oh, what I'd give for a tasty fresh French peach!

Smoking

As I sit here and write this, 49 people will needlessly die. Every 74 seconds a person passes away from smoking or smoke-related illness.

A quote in a recent edition of *Smokers' Advocate* goes like this: "Smokers, hold your heads up high and continue to enjoy one of life's greatest pleasures."

The smoker who wrote those "inspirational" words will give up at least eight years of his or her life to continue this addictive habit. Can one third of all adults in this country be so blind?

I owned a Stop Smoking Center for years and saw it all: the triple bypasses on young men, the missing limbs, high blood pressure, bronchial problems, and more. The magazine conveniently forgets to mention the 430,000 annual fatalities that result from "life's greatest pleasure."

American tradition is based on freedom of choice. Smoke if you choose. At least 5,000 new smokers are needed daily to keep the tobacco industry happy and prosperous. They are appealing to the young and gullible, the naive and the followers.

Is it possible the government wants these people to keep smoking so they can save money on Social Security benefits? Since the government subsidizes the tobacco industry, it would seem as though that might be a valid point. Or are they just blind in Washington? We already know they can be deaf and dumb to the wishes of their constituents.

So here we are again at the same impasse. Low self-esteem in the nurturing years leads to acceptance of peer pressure. Kids smoke if the people they admire smoke.

I'm back on the treadmill. Help kids develop healthy self-images. Start when they are young so their character can develop properly. Don't let them become a national statistic.

*May You
Bloom
Where You
Are Planted*

No Tomorrow

There is no tomorrow. Tomorrow is here. It is called today. Today is yesterday's tomorrow. Therefore, we should plan for tomorrow but concentrate on today with its challenges and opportunities.

There is a saying: "Never put off until tomorrow what you can do after tomorrow." It is my personal philosophy that if you are in charge of the next few minutes, you will be in charge of your life. Life is made up of minutes which add up to weeks, months and years.

In the same way, short range goals add up to long range plans, on which career success is based. If you spend your time dwelling on tomorrow and the ramifications, you've missed the point—and today.

As the playwright William Congreve wrote: "Defer not till tomorrow to be wise, tomorrow's sun to thee may never rise."

He may be right, but it's not positive thinking. In any case, the idea is to be productive in today's light, not tomorrow's.

Even the classical sages of India knew about the powers of the moment when they wrote:

... yesterday is but a Dream,
and tomorrow is but a Vision.
But today well lived makes every yesterday
a dream of happiness
and every tomorrow a vision of Hope.
Look well therefore to this day.

Whether you are a sales manager, supervisor, secretary, writer, actor or homemaker, you must plan your future goals. You must also recognize that goals can only be reached one day at a time.

Use each day wisely, and for your sake *enjoy it!*

This Is Progress?

When I was dating in the 1950s, I lived in Brooklyn and had no problem using the subway to pick up my date in the Bronx. We then rode back to Manhattan to see a movie and afterwards took the subway back to her house. At three in the morning I'd be back on the train heading home to Brooklyn. The subways were clean, safe, and nobody was sleeping in the cars or on the platform—at least not yet.

These days commuters take their lives in their hands and off-rushhour riders fare even poorer. The trains and stations are filthy and filled with vagrants. New York City is not the only victim of this so-called progress.

A few days ago I watched as workmen put up a barbed wire fence around a new senior citizen community center in Coram—a quiet town on Long Island where I have lived peacefully for 14 years. The center even has its own security shack.

When I first moved here there were Deer Crossing signs at one end of the property. Potato farms prospered. Now the area abounds with companies selling anti-theft devices. I no longer feel safe walking at night and everything must be kept under lock and key. Crime is rampant and poverty is growing faster than our Gross National Product. Guns are more abundant than drivers' licenses.

I teach and preach leaving the past behind and forging ahead, yet I know we all have pleasant memories of bygone days—like mine of the formerly clean and enjoyable subway rides.

While I can remember the good old days, I certainly choose not to live them again. Hope springs eternal, I can only pray that we will be able to turn America around and set her back on safe and clean tracks.

Pet Peeves

Have you seen the cartoon of *Ziggy* passing a store with a display in the window labeled "Pet Peeves $19.95"? The box has strange looking birds peeking out.

I interpret the sketch as showing how we turn peeves into pets and treat them as family members, grooming them and taking them with us. Eventually they grow stronger and take over our lives. Then they lead *us* around.

The dictionary says a peeve is a resentment or particular grievance. Why would we want to cling to them or make them into pets? Resentments are negative energies that make us dysfunctional and paralyzed in varying degrees, unable to function anywhere close to our full capacities.

The answer is simple: Take your pet peeve out for a walk and lose it! Leave it outside your life. Eventually you can replace it with a warm fuzzy pet that will give unconditional love.

Ziggy makes us chuckle for two reasons; First, we identify with his neurotic thought patterns, and second we all know someone just like him.

Just remember this. *Ziggy* is made up and your pet peeves are real. They are part of you until you let them go. When you are free of them, it will feel as though a great weight has been lifted from your shoulders. Your frustration and anger levels will drop and you will be able to laugh more freely.

"Do all the good you can
By all the means you can
In all the ways you can
In all the places you can
At all the times you can
To all the people you can
As long as ever you can."

JOHN WESLEY'S RULE

I Miss the Young Me

Ever notice how people flock around a baby carriage eager to inspect its contents? What is this strange attraction for babies? All they do is throw up, cry, spit up and soil their diapers. But don't get me wrong—I love babies.

Part of the mystique is *innocence.* Their faces are unlined with worry, they are not riddled with guilt. I believe we envy them since they will be coddled and comforted for years without a care in the world.

I miss my original innocence. I miss the trust I had in others and the wrinkleproof face I kept for years. I miss who I was before my parents, teachers and peers began to rubber stamp their ideas on my vulnerable mind. I miss not having been taught at an early age to "know myself" as the wise ancient Greeks taught their youngsters.

Somewhere deep down inside me lies the real me. I would like to contact it at will—returning to my innocent days. It feels as though I have spent most of my adult life unraveling the psychological sweaters others have knit for me. It is a tiresome chore, mentally exhausting.

When I arrived at Ellis Island from French Morocco I had to be dewormed and deloused so I could enter America clean. It would have been nice if they could also have deprogrammed my mind to make sure I was emotionally unimpaired. I kept my refugee mentality long after the war was over, feeling the world owed me a living.

Many years passed before I realized that I was responsible for my new life, that I had to stake my own claim.

If only the innocence of our childhood could somehow be maintained as we grow more worldly-wise.

Ban the Ban

Here's a good one: A major car manufacturer wants to ban deodorants in the paint section of its factory because some of it flakes off and falls on the unfinished cars, damaging the paint.

What about the people who wear the stuff year after year—what about the damage to them?

In reality, the human body is more likely to suffer from the effects of aluminum chloride than the cars. Where are our priorities?

This great country of ours knowingly and willingly promotes products that are harmful to humans, animals and plants. The underlying theory is pursuit of profit, rather than pursuit of happiness. It doesn't matter who gets hurt.

Most of us trust big business to give us products that can be used safely. I hope this trust is justified, but I doubt it.

In my never-ending optimism, I look forward to a reawakening of the national conscience and a return to old-fashioned values where manufacturers feel a moral responsibility toward the products they produce.

In order to maintain peace of mind, I think it is important to analyze what we do. If our first priority is to make sure the consumer is being treated fairly, we, in turn, should be able sleep peacefully. And we never know where the other shoe may fall.

Do you remember the movie a few years ago about the doctor who treated his patients with contempt and ill manners? It wasn't until he developed cancer himself and became the patient that he saw how he had been acting. He was appalled at his own insensitivity.

In thinking about the ban on Ban, I wonder how the executives will like visiting the paint department after the ban has been enforced and workers are sweating away hour after hour with no deodorant. I think I'll buy some stock in a nose clip company!

DMS and MMS

Here I go with my acronyms again. The first is Dual Marriage Syndrome for those who have been married twice. The second is Multiple Marriage Syndrome—of which I am a casualty.

Each marriage which results in divorce leaves much to be desired. For a long time I was matrimonially impaired.

When my first marriage ended I was a full-blown workaholic filled with guilt. Sacrifice was my middle name. I was a living breathing martyr. I sabotaged my relationship by working harder for my sales awards than at keeping my marriage intact. It was too late when I realized where my heart should have been. Praise from the corporate world could not replace the appreciation I yearned for at home.

My second attempt failed when I became a People Pleaser instead of being true to myself. I married the woman my parents wanted me to—a teacher who was paid a full year's salary yet had two months off in the summer. They never got over that wonderful perk. My rebound marriage went the way of the first one. However, "once bitten twice shy" was not to be my philosophy.

I tried a third time but was again unsuccessful in finding the happiness for which I yearned.

My fourth and final marriage is exactly that—final! It must be a 100 percent commitment to make it work, not a 50-50 proposition as I once treated it.

One lesson I have learned from this multi-wedding thing is that you must accept people as they are, love them unconditionally, and not spend time and energy changing them. This has been a hard lesson for me since so much of our personalities are wrapped around fragile egos, the phony self we use as a shield against the outside world.

These days divorce is much bigger business than marriage. I don't want to go that route again. Been there, done it.

I now understand that there are great lessons to be learned in all relationships and I chose to learn mine now, while I am still young enough to enjoy the interplay.

TEARS

One of my favorite operas of all time is Puccini's *Tosca*. It can move me to tears. I find it interesting that humans can shed tears at both happy and sad occasions—weddings and funerals. There must be a connection here.

I have a friend who sheds more tears at children's movies than Niagara Falls, yet he keeps his emotions in check at all other times.

Tears serve as nature's eye cleaners. Every time we cry we "see" the world in a different light.

Tears also serve as a release of passion. I think men should take advantage of this instead of bottling things up inside like my friend, then exploding at inappropriate times. Women are luckier since they have no problem letting the tears flow. What a great liberator.

This quote from John Keats almost moved me to tears.

Shed no tear! O shed no tear!
The flower will bloom another year.
Weep no more! O weep no more!
Young buds sleep in the root's white core.

To which I add, weep away if it makes you feel better!

Pro Bono

Want to feel better about yourself? The best medicine is to become outer-directed in your activities and watch your inner turmoil disappear. Since the mind can only concentrate on one problem at a time, you replace offending thoughts by helping others solve *their* dilemmas.

Pro bono work is done free of charge. The term is used mainly when attorneys take on charity cases and don't charge the client.

I had occasion to do a "freebie" for a group of high school teens who were studying personal values and self-esteem. Through their outer bravado, I could sense their fears, doubts and anxieties. They have major problems and life decisions facing them: sex, careers, smoking, peer pressure, drugs, drinking, parental control, etc.

I was reminded of a study that found that teens today are less prepared to cope with life than their parents were a generation ago. In spite of antibiotics and vitamins, they are less healthy and less cared for than any previous generation. The average age of first-time drug users is 13. The teen homicide rate has increased two and a half times; teen pregnancy has multiplied *six times* to over one million per year. Suicide has become the second leading cause of death.

At a time when values are considered opinions, moral restraint has become a dead issue. The result is a breakdown of character. Many teens are coping with despair, dissolution of families, anger, hatred and frustration with society.

The school I visited had locked doors, barred windows and security guards—not much different from a prison. The students are virtual prisoners. Then they go home to what many consider another prison, with parental rules and regulations galore. They are increasingly unable to deal with the fast-changing world and its values.

The students did not understand why I would lecture for *free*. Nobody does anything for free, they told me. When I told them my payment was the thanks I would receive from them, they still did not understand.

Frankly, for once I could not blame them.

"We have no more right to consume happiness without producing it than to consume wealth without producing it."

GEORGE BERNARD SHAW

"To make headway, improve your head."

B. C. FORBES

You Can't Go Home Again

Fifty years ago Thomas Wolfe wrote a book with that title. And isn't it the truth?

In 1986 I was visiting Brussels, Belgium, where I was born. I headed toward the old section of the city which I had last seen on May 14, 1940 when the Nazis were threatening to bomb it.

I found the building where we lived, but it was boarded up and I could not get in. It was just an old, decrepit, broken-down structure that bore no resemblance whatsoever to what my family once called home. I took a few pictures then moved on, disappointed that I experienced no emotion.

The following day I flew to Israel to visit a cemetery outside Tel Aviv where my father was buried. My brother met me there so we could pay our final respects together. It was a bittersweet moment for both of us.

The trip served a useful purpose for me. It closed a part of the past that was still open and hurting. I always lecture that living in the past robs us of the present. However, sometimes we need closure. I have yet to return to Casablanca where we spent three traumatic years and put that place to rest in my mind.

Meanwhile, I'll continue to enjoy living on Long Island in the present, not the past or the future, and relishing every moment.

Unweaving Baskets

In a Brussels hotel lobby I saw a sign posted that read: "The lift is being fixed for the next day. During that time we regret that you will be unbearable."

While this struck me funny at the time, unbearable seems to be a word that requires a bit more study.

Forty years ago the American Psychiatric Association had defined 110 psychological disorders. Today that number has increased to 210. Technology and mental health are diverging; the more we gain materially, the less we can cope with daily stress.

As a nation we are riding a guilt trip of major proportions which causes millions of us to self-destruct. The statistics are alarming.

- One-third of all Americans smoke
- One-quarter are overweight
- Two-thirds drink
- 28 million use illegal drugs

These self-punishing habits are the breeding grounds for mental illness. I call it weaving baskets—using tranquilizers, liquor and drugs as a way to cope.

George Bernard Shaw once wrote: "Better keep yourself clean and bright; you are the window through which you must see the world."

To do this we must learn to feel good about ourselves. We must dump the inferiority complexes that most of us carry around and start unweaving the old baskets of guilt and indecision.

I did not have time to hang around Brussels until the elevator was fixed and I became "bearable" again. But I have been on a lifelong crusade to help others learn to bear their burdens without abusing their bodies with drugs, drink or tobacco.

It is important not to attach too much importance to life's little setbacks. Think of the ups and downs as an elevator ride. If the lift is down, it must go back up.

Halfway

Today marks six months since I began this manuscript. As I sit back and review what I have written, and re-evaluate some of the resolutions I made back in January, I think it will make an interesting vignette. So here goes.

Most resolutions are made in sand. They are based on doing or not doing things differently from the way we did them in the past.

We promise to work harder, exercise more, relax, eat healthier foods, be kinder, read self-help books. We promise not to overeat, curse, lose our temper, neglect our families, smoke or drink to excess—all noble virtues. But I'll bet if you made any of these resolutions on January 1, you've already broken at least some of them.

Why? Because you're missing the point. Instead of the do/don't philosophy, you should be concentrating on the be/am point of view. Instead of worrying and trying to change what we do externally, we should try to become self-actualized.

Don'ts are negatives; being or becoming is a positive step in the right direction. The Greeks called it *apocatastasis* (don't try to pronounce it!). It means renewing or restoring one's mind. Fill the mind with positive happenings, use them to fuel your attitude for the new year.

Forget your resolutions and vow to improve your daily existence instead.

2,500 Years of Self-Help

To visualize is to imagine or see in the mind's eye. When you vitalize what you visualize, you bring it to life.

To give a concrete example, I have taken quotes from two masters, Lao-tzu (604-531 B.C.) and Samuel Smiles, who wrote a self-help book in 1859.

"A journey of a thousand miles must begin with a single step," wrote Lao-tzu.

Smiles' insight was that "Earnest resolution has often seemed to have about it almost a savor of impotence."

Although 2,500 years separate these great minds, their ideas formulate into a powerful single idea.

Most of the concepts of today are actually old forgotten ones. There are few new and different notions under the sun (technology excluded). As Carl Jung explained, we are all interconnected in the collective unconscious enabling us to think anything that has been thought of before and use it in different combinations.

Personal growth takes place when we can imagine *purposeful* goals and work our way toward them. Self-help requires going back inside ourselves and tapping our unconscious mind for ways to move us ahead in life.

If you dig long enough, you will surely come up with wise and wonderful thoughts.

Happy reflecting.

Dead Right

He who seeks revenge should dig two graves. That old Chinese proverb is wise indeed.

Do you:

- Carry guilt?
- Hold a grudge?
- Run scared?
- Walk a tightrope?
- Nurture hatred?
- Nurse anger?

If so, you are loaded down with negative energy. Would you rather be dead right than alive and healthy? Since the best defense is a strong offense, we maintain our fragile egos by attacking others.

Ego is defined as "the self, especially when contrasted with another self." Since this self is made up of millions of imprints left by others, the resulting self is made up of positive and negative data. Unfortunately, too much is contrary.

Psychologists tell us that the average five-year-old has been programmed with over 15,000 reasons not to feel good about him or herself. These mini-digs at our psyche add up forming a formidable wall behind which we hide our true selves.

The answer lies in restructuring our damaged egos by using positive affirmations, thinking good thoughts and filtering out the adverse data which bombards us daily.

Peace of mind is the final result.

"The ability to accept responsibility is the measure of the man."

ROY L. SMITH

"The truth is more important than the facts."

FRANK LLOYD WRIGHT

Mother's Day

I'd like to ban Mother's Day. Wait, before you stone me, let me explain. Mothers should be honored every day, not just once a year.

What really bothers me is the hypocrisy—we can take mothers for granted all year as long as we pay homage once a year. Kids and husbands who browbeat (and physically beat) mom go through the motions for an afternoon before returning to their old ways. Likewise, mothers who tyrannize their offspring (and spouses) now await their due: flowers, gifts and dinner out. This isn't a show of love. Nobody benefits except the retailers with their syrupy cards and restaurants with their brandy Alexanders and grasshoppers.

Retailers love this day; they created it. Then they offer sales on toasters, can openers, irons, coffee makers, waffle irons—all designed to keep mom in the kitchen, working.

If we had to pay our mothers for all the selfless things she does during the year, we couldn't afford her. On an average day the average mom is a cook, laundress, chauffeur, gardener, psychologist, lover, nurse, dietitian, housekeeper and, if she has a job outside the house, wage earner.

Isn't it better that our actions let her know how we feel all the time, instead of a yearly bribe? As husbands, we should show respect and appreciation whenever we have the opportunity. Flowers for no reason are always a treat; so is dinner out. And it wouldn't hurt to wash our own dirty laundry now and then.

POW!

Planned Optimism Works. That's POWer in action. When optimism is rooted in belief it gets the job done. Inspiration alone cannot be expected to work.

"If you keep saying things are going to be bad, you have a good chance of being a prophet," said Nobel Prize winner and author, Isaac Bashevis Singer.

If you are a member of the Self-Critics Club, get rid of your card fast. Every day is a new beginning—a chance at personal rebirth with new possibility for happiness. Optimists are generally more relaxed than pessimists. They aren't waiting for the sky to fall like Chicken Little. They show greater appreciation, compassion and enthusiasm for others.

Optimists earn more; they live longer and healthier lives. But the naysayers are always around to spread their negativity. Here's what was said about some of the most prolific and famous people in history.

- You must not set your sights too high for him (about Woodrow Wilson).
- She'll never write anything for popular consumption (about Louisa May Alcott).
- You have no voice (about Enrico Caruso).
- He is a poor student, mentally slow, unsociable and always daydreaming (about Albert Einstein).
- He asks foolish questions (about Abraham Lincoln).
- Her interests in daredevil projects are just not fitting for a young lady (about Amelia Earhart).

Heard enough? Well, here's one more example to prove a point.

The "victim" was Victor Seribriakoff. At age 15 his teacher told him he was a moron and suggested he quit school. He followed her poor advice and worked at manual labor until the age of 32 when he took an intelligence test. He scored 161—at the genius level. Victor began to act like the intellect he was. He wrote books, invented gadgets and became a successful entrepreneur. The only thing that changed Victor from a victim to a victorious businessman was his change of mind, his self-image.

Birthday Boy

Today is my birthday and I will make this short and sweet so I can take the day off and spend time enjoying this beautiful spring day.

I believe we only have one birth day—the day we are born. All celebrations thereafter are anniversaries of our birth.

Personally I think we make too big a deal of birthdays, with all the hoopla. A modest party is all right for kids. They love to know they are appreciated, but large ornate parties make those who cannot afford similar ones feel less worthy than their more affluent peers. So right from the beginning those feelings of inferiority creep in.

As an adult, I do not like being reminded that old age is creeping up on me. I take every day as it comes. Turning the corner at 30 or 40 or 60 makes the passage of time seem ominous—as though it's the doomsday countdown. Those hideous questions, "How does it feel to be half a century old?" make it even worse.

So I'd like to propose a toast on the anniversary of my birth: "Here's to health and happiness and a good living at any age. And please don't ask how old I am!"

Discomfort Zone

Most of us live our lives in a discomfort zone—the area where we feel safe and secure. No, I didn't make a mistake. I believe we are really uncomfortable living in a structured environment year after year. Instead of making the most of what we are born with, we barely scratch the surface of our potential.

As children, we begin walking by tottering round. Every time we encounter negativity, it bogs us down until it feels as though our feet are encased in concrete. The older we get, the heavier the weights become until we become rooted in the discomfort zone. What we really want to do is break loose and fly.

What keeps us from fulfilling ourselves is simply fear. We've been raised with doubt, distrust, and insincerity as the cornerstones of our psyche.

Here's a challenge. Before the next month is over, I'd like you to take the first step toward casting off the cement boots that are holding you down. Make a vow to get rid of at least one negative emotion that you've been carrying around since the beginning of time.

I promise you'll feel lighter than air.

How's Your PC?

I'm not referring to your personal computer but to your Prosperity Consciousness.

As I sit here writing this, more than 5 trillion chemical operations are occurring every second in my brain! No computer could work that efficiently. So how can any of us walk around with low self-esteem?

Low self-esteem translates to lack of motivation, which in turn makes us ill prepared to deal with life.

There's an old saying, "Luck is a crossroad where preparation and opportunity meet."

There's another saying, the Boy Scouts' motto: "Be prepared."

Are you prepared? Are you ready to meet life's emergencies and life's opportunities? If you answered no, better get with the program because life will pass you right by.

Remember the old carousel with the brass ring that you could grab as your horse went around? Life is just like that.

To be prepared, keep an open mind to what's going on around you. If a chance to improve or better yourself or your financial situation arises, take advantage of the opportunity. We will soon be coming to the halfway point of this year. Have you given up any golden chances so far? Are you staying at your level of achievement because you are afraid to reach out for the brass ring, afraid of failure or rooted in cement?

It takes guts to change. But only through taking chances can your Prosperity Consciousness make any headway. With all those trillions of chemical interactions going on, I'm sure you will soon realize that you can do anything you put your mind to.

"Despise not thy mother when she is old."

PROVERBS 23:22

"If we abide by the principles taught by the Bible, our country will go on prospering."

DANIEL WEBSTER

Writing

Why do I love to write? I believe writing can be the most powerful, personal, permanent and effective way to communicate.

Writing is powerful when its purpose is to incite, excite, exhilarate, aggravate or frustrate—in other words, touch us.

Writing is personal when used as a one-on-one tool to express intimate thoughts and share insights. Some writers allow others to "walk into their minds" and explore. Why would anyone "let it all hang out" like that? Writing provides a wonderful release from the ghosts that haunt us.

The beauty of writing is its permanence. We are still benefitting from the timeless gems of masters and sages long gone. We can still enjoy the classics written hundreds of years ago.

Good writing unites writer and reader with an artistic cord, strong yet invisible. Human emotions are shared; time, space and physical barriers are transcended.

Writing can be used to hurt or heal. The power lies in the ability of certain words to make us feel good or bad about ourselves and the situations in which we are involved. Imaginative blending of verbs, adjectives and metaphors can impact upon us and make us prod our own psyches for answers to questions that have been nagging at us.

Words without emotion leave the reader feeling cheated. To touch others, writers must dig down into their souls and root out the passion, allowing it to surface in the form of words. Not an easy task, I assure you. Reading the words of others can provide the stimulus that leads to instant insights about our own problems—the "aha" experience.

Shakespeare put it best when he wrote in *Hamlet:*

My words fly up, my thoughts remain below:
Words without thoughts never to heaven go.

Write on!

News

Headline: No Airline Crashes
Headline: No Fatalities During Rush Hour
Headline: Our Streets Are Safe

How long would these bland news headlines hold your attention? Not long I bet. You'd be skimming the text for juicier tidbits filled with blood and guts, murder and mayhem. I make it my business to read the comics first so that my mental outlook will be *positive*. Then I read the headlines, usually skipping the gore which comprises most of the paper. Why do I even bother reading it? To remain current.

Newsday published a 32-page supplement to commemorate the 50th anniversary of the bombing of Pearl Harbor. What an awful reminder of war. The articles in the special certainly stirred up old angers in millions of people whose lives were affected directly or indirectly by the horrors of World War II. Why punish our psyches by reliving the angst so many of us suffered years ago?

Remembering the past, including the loss of loved ones, is important. But we should try to keep anger from creeping into our thoughts or else we perpetuate the prejudice and hatred of those who are different than we are.

Because of religious persecution, I spent my eighth birthday running from the Nazis. Others were not so lucky. Those who remember the "good old days" are generally suffering from a poor memory. Please check yours.

Generation Chasm

I recently finished reading a survey taken for *Teen* magazine. The results were quite unsettling. The teenage boys ranked their female counterparts as "cool" if they were:

- Interested in him
- Loyal to him
- Considerate and thoughtful of him

Talk about adolescent insecurities. Down at the bottom of the list were assertiveness and intelligence. I guess they don't count for much in adolescence. What a me-me-me mentality. The modern liberated girl ranked a lowly 16th in the survey.

When asked what they thought girls liked in them, the boys answered: good looks and muscular builds. Intelligence didn't even make the top 10.

With this highly distorted sense of values being programmed into this new generation, the following facts are not surprising:

- Ten million juveniles are in the criminal justice system
- Fourteen million young adults are emotionally disturbed

Parents often feel that teachers should be stressing ethics and morality. Teachers are too stressed just trying to impart the information necessary for graduation. Values must be taught at *home*. What's right, what's important and what's wrong must be learned at an early age.

Getting back to the survey, youngsters need to learn that looks don't count for everything. Young men should be advised that a strong, intelligent woman will make them more successful. Young women will learn later in life that a well-muscled body doesn't stay that way. They will learn (hopefully not too late) that a quick mind and keen imagination are the tickets to leading a healthy and productive life.

I can only hope my son Joseph can see beyond the curves, seductive smiles and shiny hair of his female classmates when he starts seriously dating. I hope I have taught him well. My fingers are crossed.

How about you? Have you instilled your children with honest values and a decent work ethic? Have you taught them to respect the opposite sex? If not, you have your work cut out for you.

TV or Not TV

Is it nobler in the mind to suffer the slings and arrows of outrageous television, or to take arms against a sea of visual garbage? (I hope Shakespeare forgives my taking such liberties with his words of wisdom.)

The idea came to me as I watched five women who were engrossed in a soap opera during their lunch break. As they discussed the plot I was struck by the way they treated the characters as real. These women, aged 19 to 65, seem to have lost their grip on reality.

The women worked for a large company in the customer service department. I could certainly understand their wanting to get away from brash and whining customers for a while. But surely there must be a better way to spend a lunch hour than to indulge in this modern mythology called the soaps.

My reason for being there was to observe and recommend ways to improve their successful contact ratio with irate customers. In order to succeed I had to touch a nerve in all of them based on the desire to reduce their job stress.

Unlike the fantasy of soap operas, real people love to dump on customer service reps. Of course, without these complainers, these five women (and others just like them) would be out of a job.

My suggestion would first be to get these women out of the imaginary world of television and into new techniques of dealing with people, including patience, respect, empathy and enthusiasm.

Unless they get a grip on reality, they will not be able to effectively deal with real people and their real problems. They will be waiting for their "shining knight" to come rescue them from the daily ranting and ravings of dissatisfied clients.

So, ladies, turn off the television and tune into the real world. If you follow these techniques, you'll see it is a much better place to be.

Sex and Statistics

An intriguing piece in a financial newsletter caught my attention. The article stated, among other things, that the average American has sex 57 times per year. That odd number got me thinking.

I can count the first 52 times—that would be once a week. After that, perhaps sex on the birthday of each partner. That makes 54.

If you add in New Year's Eve (always a good time to celebrate) that makes it 55. But what about the other two?

We can throw in Valentine's Day and a wedding anniversary celebration to bring the number to 57. Well, it makes for a lively discussion, but are the figures real or fake?

Although I love statistics I do not trust them. For instance, the American family has an average of 1.7 children. Figure that one out.

At my age, statistically I have a chance of living another 23 years. But if a car mows me down tomorrow, will someone else have gained my 23 years? Will it affect the statistics for the future?

I guess the point here is to take everything with (pardon the cliche) a grain of salt. Try not to put too much faith into anything you hear—or even see. The eyes can play tricks too.

Instead trust in yourself and your own *inner feelings* of right and wrong, good and bad, up and down.

A Rose by Any Other Name…

"A man is rich in proportion to the things he can afford to let alone."

HENRY DAVID THOREAU

"By working faithfully eight hours a day, you may eventually get to be a boss and work 12 hours a day."

ROBERT FROST

Roses

When is a rose not a rose? When you're thinking about it. It becomes a rose when you begin to *feel* it is a rose. Confused? Let me explain.

A few years ago I attended a three-day seminar on the new science of hemisphericity (the brain and its bicameral functions). The highlight came on the last day when the facilitator asked us to draw a rose. Most of our results were dismal. There were not a dozen decent drawings in a room of 150 people!

Undaunted, the facilitator guided us into a long meditation. She led us into a forest of roses with stems 30 feet tall. She had us climb the roses and inhale deeply, admiring the color and texture. We had left our thinking side (left brain) behind on this journey and experienced only the feeling side (right brain). The results were miraculous. Almost every one of us was able to produce a second set of drawings fit to be framed. I kept mine for years as a reminder of the experiment or whenever I needed to tap into my imaginative, intuitive and inspirational side, ergo the right brain.

If you can't stop to smell the roses because time is too precious, smell them in your mind. Let the right (feeling) side take over for a while and you'll feel refreshed, ready to tackle new projects. This concept works in reverse for left-handers.

Whenever I need a mental "fix" I retire into my inner space where I am not limited by time and physical constraints. I relax and smell the roses. Why don't you try it?

Negative Faith

Did you know pharmaceuticals are the most profitable industries in the world? They are followed closely by the tobacco and liquor industries. Is anyone surprised? The biggest money-maker in the world consists of providing drugs designed to alleviate the problems caused by smoking and drinking. Talk about an unholy trio.

Smoking, drinking and taking drugs never solves anything. What *we believe* we are determines *what* we are. Misguided faith, backed by low self-image, controls our lives. That is why there are those who:

- Stay poor no matter how many financial breaks they get
- Stay sick even with the best medical care
- Stay fat even when they diet
- Remain lonely even when surrounded by others
- Complain even though they are rich

True faith, backed by the unconditional belief that we are born to be better, *not bitter,* will eliminate the need for drugs, drinks and smokes. And a guided faith, backed by confidence, will allow us to:

- Get rich in spite of recessions
- Remain healthy whether or not we see a doctor
- Stay slim even when eating junk foods
- Find love in the right places
- Lead happy lives though financially lacking

The Gap

"If we take people as they are we make them worse," said Johann W. von Goethe. "If we treat them as if they were what they ought to be, we help them to become what they are capable of being."

If only we could remember that and apply it to our daily lives it would certainly help end disagreements and arguments.

While old studies showed that man's nature was inherently violent, more recent findings indicate that it is scientifically incorrect to say that humans have a "violent" brain. The inventors of war can become the inventors of peace. Let's put the theory of natural aggressiveness in man to rest once and for all, thus closing the gap between theory and reality.

Which brings us to another dilemma. What excuse do men have for continuing the insane wars that are always breaking out somewhere? What makes them think that social and economic problems can be solved with war?

My experiences as a child gave me an aversion to conflict of any kind. Once we realize war accomplishes nothing, we can concentrate on the human potential. The greatest goal the United Nations can have is to bridge the gap between what humans are today and what they can become tomorrow. Only then will we know what "Love thy neighbor" means.

Here's what some of the great thinkers of yesterday and today say about war:

- "When women have a voice in national and international affairs, war will cease forever." (Augusta Stowe-Gullen)
- "If men recognize no law superior to their desires, then they must fight when their desires collide." (R. H. Tawney)
- "In a modern war you will die like a dog for no good reason." (Ernest Hemingway)
- "What difference does it make to the dead?" (Mahatma Gandhi)
- "There never was a time when, in my opinion, some way could not be found to prevent the drawing of the sword." (Ulysses S. Grant)

Singles

It has been 10 years since I gave my last singles talk, so I was unprepared for what I recently heard and saw. A decade ago most of the singles I lectured to were high on life. Now they have a beaten look and attitude. The women, especially, appear haunted and desperate. They exchange dating horror stories. I have to wonder where the blame really lies.

In studying the schedule of events, I noted that they were all designed for fun, fun, fun, instead of connecting with the right person. My talk entitled "How to Attract and Develop a Loving Relationship" was the only event designed to prevent the loneliness they seemed to be experiencing.

To make my talk interesting I used the acronym for SINGLES (pardon me, I can't help myself). It goes like this (hum a tune if you feel inclined):

S is for *sincerity* in all relationships.
I is for being the *individual* you are.
N is for *networking*, an important process to meet the right people.
G is for *guilt*. Eliminate it.
L is for *love*, which we all want.
E is for *enthusiasm;* allow it to come out and play.
S is for *selling* yourself and your ideas to others.

Indulge me for one more minute while I add the acronym LIFE:

L is for *laughing* and *lightening* up.
I is for *inspiration* and *imagination*, which makes relationships grow and blossom.
F is for *friends*, make them and keep them.
E is for *excellence* in all you attempt.

Toilet Paper

This may be an odd topic for a book on positive attitudes but stick with me for a moment while I express myself.

The toilet paper in our master bathroom came dangerously close to pink. When I asked my (previous) wife about it, she said it was peach. Our son agreed that it was peach. I was outvoted.

So I began to take my business downstairs to the black and white bathroom where the toilet paper was, mercifully, white. I once tried sneaking a roll of blue onto the holder but as soon as my wife noticed, it was back to peach (pink).

Call it a macho thing if you want, but I think toilet paper should be neutral—neither a masculine nor a feminine color. I'm no doubt overreacting, going against all the virtues that I hold sacred, but I don't feel I'm asking for too much. Just *white* toilet paper. That's all. Anybody agree?

"We must cultivate our garden."

VOLTAIRE

*"I am an idealist. I don't know where I'm going
but I'm on my way."*

CARL SANDBURG

Suicide

Books on suicide are becoming number-one bestsellers; they are featured in the weekly news magazines.

I have a problem with this. I worry over terms such as "unbearable suffering," which can be purely emotional in nature, with no physical pain attached. We all have pain and emotional problems. That doesn't mean we should all run out and kill ourselves.

Chapters in these suicide instruction manuals include:

- How Do You Get the Magic Pills?
- Going Together (for couples who want to split from life as an alternate vacation plan).
- Self-deliverance via the Plastic Bag (for sanitary types).

It only costs $20 for a seriously depressed person to pick up a copy and find out exactly how to do *it*. It's a sad commentary on our society that the authors of these books garner such publicity while the real heroes, the therapists and psychologists who help reduce the feelings of despair and hopelessness, are neglected.

Suicide is permanent. Once completed, there's no going back. Instead of contemplating the "deed," why not spend $20 on a holistic healing book, a self-help tape, a seminar that concentrates on good feelings?

We're all on a slow suicide ride no matter what, with all the chemically infested food and drinks we ingest. I, for one, am in no hurry to rush things along by doing myself in.

Wishbone or Backbone

Wishbone people go through life allowing things to happen *to* them. They are dreamers and often victims of circumstance.

Backbone individuals *make* things happen. They are victors, the doers and self-made successes.

Many might consider my family victims since we ran from the Nazis. But I feel that experience gave us all backbones. My parents were brought up with the concepts of honesty, integrity, respect for others and they passed those values down to my brother and me.

Parents these days don't seem to have the time to pass adequate values on to their children. They cannot instill the backbone needed for their offspring to deal with life adequately so they become wishbone people, waiting to see *what* will happen, instead of making it happen.

Where does this lead? Down the road, children wake up and realize they've been shortchanged.

"Children begin by loving their parents," wrote Oscar Wilde. "After a time they judge them. Rarely, if ever, do they forgive them."

Most parents do their best based on their own feelings as victim or victor. But parents are not without their own faults. If you have picked up the victim status from your role models, it can be changed around by forgiveness. By finally accepting and understanding what your mother and father are, while not following in their footsteps, you can turn your wishbone philosophy around and acquire a backbone at last.

Plague

There is a plague called the Chronic Complainer Syndrome. As we know from research, humans need to feel *important.* Notice that when you talk, you probably rant on about yourself. We start conversations bragging about our accomplishments, look for approval, and when we run out of good things to talk about we start complaining.

Complainers are looking for a dumping ground for their bad luck, illness, financial problems, marital woes, etc. They don't want advice, they want pity, sympathy and a willing ear to listen.

If talk is food for the brain, then repeated doses of negative talk act like small doses of poison. Enough toxic input will activate the negative energy that each of us carries around, making even the most cheerful person gloomy.

If you are pegged as that willing ear, you must learn defensive tactics. Instead of wearing a doormat that says Step on Me, try dumping your own problems on the complainer. See if that turns things around.

I listen to friends, relatives and peers who complain. But only once. I offer options, not advice, and expect that the subject is closed thereafter. If this doesn't work, I visualize them as having a plague sign on their chest and when I see them, I duck out of sight.

I like to follow the old Chinese proverb: The person who says it can't be done should not interfere with the person who is doing it.

55 mph or Bust

You drive your car on the highway and every few miles, when you see a 55 mph sigh, you stop, get out of the car and replace the sign with one that reads 1.1 mph. You get back in the car and proceed to the next sign at the new, slower speed.

If that sounds ridiculous, think about this:

At birth we are all given an innate success mechanism, a new machine that is capable of going 55 mph if both the *thinking* and *feeling* sides of our brains are working in sync. If our brain is not functioning correctly, we end up traveling at 1.1 mph.

The road to failure is paved with good intentions, and we travel over them in reckless fashion on our way to an average life.

Here's a story to illustrate: Three frogs sit on a lily pad. One decides to jump off. How many frogs are left? If you answered two you are wrong. There are still three left because one only *decided* to jump. He didn't actually do it.

Decision, not followed by action, is worthless. The same holds true for intention. Without action, they also have no value.

The word action is self-fulfilling. Scrambling the letters, I come up with I-act-on—now that makes sense. You might scramble it as I-noact. The choice is always yours.

Getting back to the speed limit, it's also your decision whether you want to travel down the road of life at a full 55 or a mere 1.1 miles per hour. Is your foot on the gas or the brake?

Terminal Boredom

Following naturally from yesterday's little lecture comes this gem.

Are you bored? Children, especially teens, always seem to be at odds to find something to do. Yet here we are in the most affluent country in the world, surrounded by books, videos, games (both the board and electronic varieties) and yet they have nothing to occupy their time.

In my childhood, reading was a gift, a treasure to be cherished.

Nowadays, few children read. Many parents are too busy to spend quality time with their youngsters; instead they encourage the electronic baby sitter (the television).

Although I've encouraged him, my son is not a reader. Give him a stack of CDs and he disappears for hours. I feel bad that he's missing the excitement of using his imagination.

You can lead a child to books but you cannot make him (her) read.

Reading by example works best if you catch young minds at the crossroads, before they are set in their ways. For me, I've found there's never a case of terminal boredom when I have a good book handy. Now excuse me, I've got to finish the chapter I'm on. Then back to reading.

"Men just don't seem to jump off the bridge for big reasons; they usually do so for little ones."

W. H. FERRY

"Often the test of courage is not to die but to live."

CONTE VITTORIO ALFIERI

"There is more treasure in books than in all the pirates' loot on Treasure Island… and best of all, you can enjoy these riches every day of your life."

WALT DISNEY

"To read without reflecting is like eating without digesting."

EDMUND BURKE

A Job Is a Job Is a Job

The California State University at Fullerton finished a 16-year study and found that of 350,000 applicants, *80 percent* were in the wrong job.

Another study done by the Marketing Survey and Research Corporation confirmed the fact that four out of five employees in the workplace were not doing what they were best suited for.

Since anger and frustration follow when one is unhappy with one's job, it is easy to understand why sickness and absenteeism are rampant.

Even worse, violence by disgruntled employees and former workers is making the workplace more like a war zone.

The people who are happy earning a living are few and far between. They do exist, however, and I have just finished reading about one. Dr. Matthew Warpick is a doctor who just celebrated his 90th birthday at his office, where he continues his medical practice six days a week. He remains in a crime-ridden neighborhood, exemplifying the highest humanitarian standards.

"The reward in this type of practice is knowing you're helping people, people who need you," says Dr. Warpick. "That keeps me alive."

Not everyone can be a 90-year-old doctor, but I firmly believe if people loved their work this would be a happier world.

Stand back and analyze how you earn your daily bread. Do you feel good about the work you do, or is there some inner yearning to do something else?

If there is, start reading the help wanted ads, sign up for a course, go back to school. Perhaps now is the time for a career change. Why spend the rest of your working years saying "What if…" or "If only I had."

A job may be just a job. But since you spend a good part of your waking hours doing it, you may as well enjoy it and turn it into a career.

Generation Gap

The past two generations have seen a tremendous growth in art, music and dance. Rock and roll—which shocked parents in the fifties—seems positively tame by today's standards. It is not unusual for rock concerts nowadays to use pyrotechnics and smoke bombs with music so loud your eardrums are blown inside out. It's a far cry from the sedate chamber music evenings of Mozart's day.

Take a look at the past and present. I'm sure you'll agree we've come a long way—for better or worse. We went from:

Bach to Bon Jovi

Bartok to Black Crows

Mozart to Madonna, etc.

With all due respect to the younger generation (of which my son is a member), we've gone from the classics to rubbish, from melody to mayhem, from literary masterpieces to romantic drivel.

The great humanitarian and Nobel prize winner, Mother Teresa, talks about *spiritual deprivation* which erodes human values. I think she could include most of America's alienated youth in her appraisal.

Spiritual hardship stems in part from lack of respect. Who are the role models of today? At one time they were the parents. But so many parents are dysfunctional, they cannot be held up as shining examples. Business leaders? Every day we read about them being arrested for scamming an unsuspecting public. Entertainers? Many live on a steady diet of drugs and alcohol. Sports figures? More drugs, wife beatings and sexual exploits to make even the most liberal minds cringe.

In the past two generations we have made such great strides in technology and medicine. If only there could be a balance between the old and the new.

I can appreciate some of the rock music played by my son, but I also love the classics by the masters. I wish he could do the same.

We should try to remain open minded. Let us try to enjoy Beethoven and the Bee Gees with the same enthusiasm. I think it will help close the generation gap.

Odd Couples

I was watching an old rerun of *The Odd Couple* when a light bulb went off in my head. It had to do with dynamic duos.

Some of the best shows on television in past years involved two people interacting: Felix and Oscar on *The Odd Couple*; Christine and Mary Beth on *Cagney and Lacy*; Sam and Diane on *Cheers*; and Edith and Archie on *All in the Family.*

The brain has two chambers, right and left. The left is the rational side, the right is the intuitive or feeling side. If we go back to the programs, we see that the producers have pitted a "left-brainer" against a "right-brainer" in each instance. And it works beautifully. The disagreements make for hilarious comedy or great conflict, both highly desirable commodities on television.

In our own minds, when the right and left sides are in conflict, we get nowhere. The rational fights the intuitive, *thinking* clashes with *feeling* causing stress and illness.

If what you think and what you feel don't work well together, you must either change your thought process or deny your feelings.

Easier said than done.

A way that works for me is to make lists.

Let's say you've been offered a job that sounds good, but something in your gut is saying don't take it. Pull out that paper and start writing.

The up side: It is something you'd like to do, it pays well, the conditions are pleasant. The down side: It is a long commute during rush hour which means wear and tear on the car, extra gas costs, frustration and anxiety as you buck traffic every day in both directions.

It's a tough call. But if the company plans to move closer to you within the next six months or if they offer you a company car and a gas expense account, the decision becomes easier. The rational and intuitive side have a better chance of meshing than clashing. In most cases, things can be worked out with a bit of clear-headed thought.

We are all "odd couples" in the cerebral department much of the time. But when the two halves of our brain cooperate there is nothing we cannot accomplish.

MYOB

Time for another acronym. MYOB, according to Ann Landers, is Mind Your Own Business. For me it stands for Mind Your Own *Beliefs*.

We all inherit a belief system at birth. It is comprised of intuition, instinct and the innate connection to Cosmic Intelligence. If we work with our belief system we can lead a productive life. As rules and regulations and other value systems are introduced, our thinking changes.

Biofeedback programs are useful tools for allowing us to return to the stage within ourselves before conditioning began taking its emotional toll. We can experience our "gut" feelings or intuitive side.

Minding your own beliefs does not mean trying to convert others to your system. As Emerson said: "What you *are* screams so loud I can't hear what you *say*."

If you wish to influence someone, become a living example, a role model. Goodness knows we have too few good ones. You'll stand out like a sore thumb.

The Cosmic Chef

I once held a three-hour workshop with a group of women telemarketers who sell ad space for a daily newspaper.

Telemarketing is one of the toughest jobs. It requires communication skills, judgment abilities, and *patience.*

When these women come into work they each bring a mental menu.

The good ones begin their shift with the appetizer, or attitude—the general demeanor and peace of mind they need before picking up the telephone for the first electronic confrontation with a prospective client or complainer.

Generally, they do well if they skip the soup and salad, which are the hard luck stories other operators tell while milling around the coffee pot.

The main course is the sales pitch, made with dignity and with all portions of information at their fingertips. Their presentation is cooked just right and they present it with a flourish of good spirit.

Dessert is the affirmation from the person contacted that they have done an excellent job and the icing on the cake is the contract for space sold.

The telemarketing chefs who keep a positive attitude do well at their jobs. None of them enjoy rejection; *nobody does.* They understand, however, that "no's" are a part of the business and they don't let it get them down.

Learn to be a cosmic chef by taking the good and the bad with equal composure. Try not to get flustered and bent out of shape when the recipe doesn't come out the way you like it. Try again, making a substitution of spirit and see if it cooks better the next time.

"A bore is a man who, when you ask him how he is, tells you."

BERT LESTON TAYLOR

"Always forgive your enemies—nothing annoys them so much."

OSCAR WILDE

"God is not a cosmic bell-boy."

HARRY E. FOSDICK

Robotics

When the late great science fiction master, Isaac Asimov, first coined the word *robotics,* he attached a set of rules to these new man-made "humanoids." The three laws for their behavior were:

1. A robot may not injure a human being or, through inaction, allow a human person to come to harm.
2. A robot must obey orders given to it by humans except when such order would conflict with the first law.
3. A robot must protect its own existence as long as such protection does not come in conflict with laws one and two.

It's fairly obvious that the above rules were written tongue-in-cheek. The rules must be what Asimov had in mind when he thought of real "humanoids" (human beings) acting like robots. I believe he was using poetic license to sneak his rules for human behavior past our psychological defenses and yet still convey the message. Change the word *robot* to *human* in the three rules outlined above and see how well it fits.

Asimov, author of more than 500 books, had a lot in common with another genius, Wolfgang AmadeusMozart. Mozart lived two centuries earlier and was also prolific—turning out over 600 musical masterpieces in his brief life. Each had a humility with regard to their special gift. Mozart believed he was the conduit through which God sent great music. Asimov said: "All I want is a working typewriter, an ample supply of paper and my library. My life wells up completely from *within.*"

Both men understood that their gifts from God were "on loan," yet they shared their immense talents with the world.

The difference between them was the time in which they lived. Mozart knew nothing about robots. He was a risk-taker and an outcast who was willing to go out on a limb with his personal philosophy. He defied tradition and, in doing so, he commanded respect of his peers.

Unfortunately, today there are more robots than risk-takers. The new young minds are blitzed by Nintendo, CDs, television, arcade games, Game Boy. There are very few freethinkers willing to put themselves on the line like Mozart and Asimov.

Dark-Light

In my motivational lectures I use the following example to show how wise the comic character Pogo is when he says: "We have met the enemy and he is us!"

When asked what needs to be pushed to light up a room, most people say "the light switch." But I have a thought for you.

If there were no light switch, the light would always be on since power would continually flow to the bulb. To stop the flow, we attach a "dark switch." The same is true with our minds.

When we are born we are connected intuitively to the collective wisdom of the ages. As we grow, the "no's" flow into our power source from parents, teachers, bosses, friends, relatives and even strangers. Every NO becomes a dark switch, shutting off a portion of the wisdom we are born with. Psychologists have indicated that we receive at least 15,000 negative messages before we reach the tender age of *five!* Yet as mature adults we are expected to use our full potential.

If you want to break out of the dark and into the light, you must unwire the dark switches which hold you back. Take away their power through an immediate and positive flow of electricity. We are born with the gift of light, we must regain control of it by feeling worthy of flipping the switch.

A final thought: Be cautious about putting dimmer switches into the innocent minds of others—your children. Let them use their Godgiven light and intuitive reasoning to become as bright as floodlights.

Love and Positive Thinking

Every day the news seems to get more violent, more bloody, more outrageous. Bad news makes people angry, anger turns to frustration, which, in turn, becomes hatred. Since we rarely attack what angers us, we disguise the rage and take it out on those closest to us. Generally that means our family—the ones we profess to love.

Psychologists tell us that we cannot love others until we love ourselves. We cannot give what we do not have. True feelings of self-love built on self-respect, self-esteem, honesty, integrity and compassiontake hard work. Most of us feel worthless about some aspect of our lives. Who, after all, is perfect?

Nobody here on Earth is perfect. So that lets us all off the hook.

Love and positive thinking can be linked together if we can unite them in our minds and hearts. The result is a low-cost way to eliminate all sorts of psychosomatic illness. After all, if we punish ourselves for our so-called sins by becoming sick, we can heal ourselves by thinking affirmatively.

My advice: Skip the bad news and concentrate on the good.

What Goes Around Comes Around

Here's a wonderful example of a self-fulfilling prophecy. One day while taking a walk I noticed a sign that read "Signs erected on this property will be removed." Sure enough, the next day it was gone.

Integrity when I was growing up was not a gray area. We all knew what was right and what was wrong. These days it seems as though the words mean different things to different people.

A workable synonym is honesty. When I was growing up my parents taught by example. Unfortunately, these days everyone is trying to get away with something. For instance:

- Speeding on the highway
- Adding on nonexisting items to business accounts
- Cheating on income tax forms
- Stealing small items at work like pens, paper, envelopes, stamps
- Using company time and the phone for personal long-distance calls
- Accepting more change from a cashier than we are due

The list is endless. Is this what we want our children to learn?

To me, lack of integrity means we feel unworthy of properly earning the things we want or need by honest labor. We compound this problem by playing out negative patterns.

With honor, however, our lives change for the better. Every action done in an honest manner weakens the low self-esteem and eventually we feel good about ourselves.

Living a virtuous life leads to improved self-respect which no illgotten gains can give us.

Finally, it gives us peace of mind which allows us to reach into our untapped potential.

Post a sign in your mind which reads: *Only honesty and integrity allowed here.* That's a self-fulfilling prophecy we can all live with.

Universal Laws

The law of the universe is quite simple: What you did in the past is what you'll do in the future.

In other words, if you like where you are in life's journey, don't change anything except your underwear! On the other hand, if you're looking for a better future, then modifications must be made. They must be consistent with what you've done in the past, where you are now, and where you want to go.

In working with a group of disgruntled customer service reps, I showed them that in order to make the work day more tolerable, they had to change, since the customers certainly wouldn't. Once they understood that they needed to put themselves in the customers' shoes, they saw that empathy was required. Not a belligerent attitude.

Some of the reps were astute and suggested that what they did for a living was just the tip of the iceberg as far as interpersonal relations go. I agreed. I told them that continuing with motivational and skill-enhancing programs would make them more productive in their present jobs and give them the qualities employers looked for when hiring for managerial positions.

Once they began breaking down the walls of communication, the reps became excited to try the new techniques at home with children, spouses, partners and friends.

A number of the reps also realized that suffering in a high-stress job is an *option,* not a *requirement.*

I have great faith that when I return for a follow-up seminar to that company, I will be pleasantly surprised to find that many of those who took my course have moved into better paying jobs and are interacting on a higher plane of communication, both at home and at work. I will surely see that those who are still customer service reps are turning the anger brought in by customers inside out—making sweet cream from sour milk.

*"Love cures people—both the ones who give it and
the ones who receive it."*

DR. KARL MENNINGER

*"Man—a reasoning rather than a reasonable
animal."*

ALEXANDER HAMILTON

Hot Stuff

The Red Phone

We all have a red phone—a hotline—like the one in the White House. Ours is found in the frontal lobe of our right brain. It is connected to the White Light, the Creator, the Universal Intelligence—any name you want to call it.

The red phone is the most wonderful communication tool ever invented. The trick to activating it is to connect our thinking brain (left side) with the feeling part (right side) where we have access to the innate wisdom of the ages.

To dial we must quiet the linear part of our mind through meditation, soothing music, yoga, repeating a mantra, etc.

Once the thinking side is at rest, the messages arrive loud and clear. These bulletins are commonly known as hunches or gut reactions. If we listen and follow the advice, we will have much greater control of our lives.

To check out the validity of this premise, try a little test: For *three weeks* listen to your intuition, follow it to the letter. Chart the results daily in a log book, noting events, reactions and emotions. When the three weeks are over, use the next three weeks to ignore your hunches. In other words, disconnect the red phone. Chart those events, reactions and emotions. I guarantee you will be much happier with the results of the first test.

If you have disconnected your red phone, ask yourself why. Unless you can give a satisfactory answer, reconnect it immediately.

Faith

Two young priests, John and Mark, met after their first sermons given in churches in adjacent towns.

"How did you make out with the collection?" asked John.

"Fine," replied Mark. "Most of my parishioners put in folded money. How about you?"

"Not so good," answered John. "I put in a coin to start the offerings and all I got was small change. How much did you start with?"

"A five-dollar bill," said Mark.

Mark had faith that his flock would follow his lead. He was right. But John was of little faith.

Faith is a tricky subject. We often put unlimited trust in complete strangers: We expect cooks will prepare healthy and tasty food, pilots will deliver us in one piece, and mechanics will service our cars without ripping us off. Yet when it comes to faith in God, *we hold back.*

We print "In God We Trust" on our dollar bills yet the dollar devalues daily. Perhaps we should reprint them to read "In God We Trust 20 Percent of the Time."

We pray, we beg, we plead, we cajole the Lord to overturn the original laws of cause and effect so things will go our way. But are we putting as much personal effort into making things right as we possibly can? Do we trust in ourselves?

Keep in mind that we are made in God's image. Meaning that even if we have confidence in him 80 percent of the time, we can trust ourselves the same.

I truly believe that when we travel the inward road, we get the best mileage.

HATE

"And ye shall hate thy neighbor as thyself."

Ugly words and yet they capture our attention. Most of us maintain hate as part of our daily existence. How else can we explain the substandard treatment we give to family, friends, peers, strangers, neighbors?

In effect, hate is a continuation of our own bad feelings about *ourselves*. Hate begets hate.

Self-forgiveness must come before we can forgive others. Positive pardoning of parents, siblings and peers must come next. But how do we start?

Make a list, and it may be a long one, of the people who have caused you harm—emotionally, physically, mentally—and concentrate on forgiving them. It is that simple. The effort will not be easy, it may take a while. Don't expect immediate results, especially if the pain has been considerable. Only by letting go of the attachment to the hurt can you free yourself from the prison you keep your mind and soul locked in.

As you work through each passion, cross the name off the list. And as you get closer to the end, your peace of mind will grow stronger and your self-respect will increase proportionately.

Remember this: As a child you are blameless. The hurtful things done to you are *not your fault*. Try not to feel responsible (or guilty) for bad things that happened when you were young. Put the blame where it should be, then forgive and move on with your life in a constructive manner.

If you continue to fill your time and energy with loathing for yourself and others, you can expect illness to ravage your body and mind. Think of hate as a form of cancer, spreading and becoming more deadly with each passing day. To free yourself of this malignancy, let go of the malice you feel.

Treat thy neighbor as you would treat yourself—with love.

Independence

Since today is the day marking America's independence, I'd like to present you with another thought on the subject of freedom.

If you think "I'm not good enough," instead of "I am a valuable person," I'd like to show you how you can achieve independence over this negative thought process.

What is the biggest obstacle to your own personal success? What is holding you back?

Is it money? Your spouse? Your parents? Your boss? Lack of education? Bad luck? Were you born under an unlucky star?

Write it down *now*.

All of us are suppressed, oppressed and repressed in some way by our environment and the people with whom we interact. Yet few of the people who are successful in life have any more intelligence, innate ability or luck than you or I.

The key is that successful people *believe in themselves.* They know they can reach the goals they have set despite all obstacles. They turn their ideas into reality.

Most of the great inventors, like Thomas Edison, failed hundreds or thousands of times until they hit upon the right formula. Persistence pays off.

If you don't believe you are good enough to succeed, you will find a thousand excuses to fail. Those excuses will alienate you from the things you want out of life and keep you from fulfilling and loving relationships.

On this Independence Day, midway through the calendar year, set yourself a new resolution: to become self-governing—to make yourself autonomous from the negativity that surrounds you.

Did you write down on a sheet of paper what is holding you back? If so, take a long hard look at it. Don't use that as a rationalization for failure. Cross it out, vow to not use it as an excuse and swear that you will become independent.

Then watch your life light up with the most dazzling display of fireworks.

Something to Chew On

Two cannibals were having lunch while exchanging their personal thoughts, as lifelong friends often do.

"I really hate my mother-in-law," says one to the other.

"That's okay," answers the friend. "Just eat the vegetables."

Corny, I know. The point is: Are you busy chewing things over and over in your mind? Are you wasting quality time on past things which you cannot change?

When we continue to occupy our minds with such so-called graffiti, it leaves little room for growth. Eating the "vegetables" only allows us to displace the old with new and refreshing thoughts.

When you leave the portion of "subtractive thinking" off your platter, you can eat healthy.

Consider constructive attitudes as vitamin supplements for those times when your energy slacks. As nutritionists will tell you, most people get all the nutrients they need from eating well-balanced meals. Translate that into mental food and you'll get the gist of this short vignette.

P.S. I learned to actually like my mother-in-law by chewing her viewpoints less and digesting them with a grain or two of salt!

"Faith in a holy cause is to a considerable extent a substitute for the lost faith in ourselves."

ERIC HOFFER

"A skeptic is a person who would ask God for his ID cards."

EDGAR A. SHOAFF

Prayer

A young priest writes to his bishop to ask for permission to smoke while he prays.

"Absolutely not!" is the emphatic reply.

A few days later another priest from the same parish writes to the bishop asking if he can pray while he smokes.

"Of course you may!" is the emphatic reply.

Prayer works best when one is praying for good things to happen instead of for things not to happen. Most people are afraid of ill health, poverty, romantic loss—the negatives. But if we turn our attention to *what we want,* instead of what we wish to avoid, day-to-day activities usually go more smoothly and on a more constructive level.

As the great Lebanese poet, Kahlil Gibran wrote: "You pray in your distress and in your need; would that you might pray also in the fullness of your joy and in your days of abundance."

Right v. Right

How often has someone said to you "I'm right. Case closed"?

The people who claim to be right, whether they are or not, have fragile egos which need constant stroking. The next time it happens you might ask: Is being right more important than *what's* right?

If you are one of these know-it-alls, know this: Being right is a dangerous practice. When you are not right—or more harshly when you are wrong—your ego takes a beating.

The world is not black and white. There are many subtle variations of gray. A person can be doing right in one situation, but that same action may be wrong in a different time and place.

I always laugh at the story of the woman who was out with her husband at the company Christmas party—a sit-down dinner in a fancy restaurant. As she was talking to others at the table, she reached over and began cutting his steak into bite-sized pieces. With a nudge from her hubby, she realized with embarrassment that she was doing what she usually did at home for the kiddies. It was the right thing to do in the privacy of her home, but not at a banquet with adults.

Most religions teach that they are the Chosen Ones. Wars have been waged throughout the ages over who is right, yet there is no "right" religion. Each of us prays in the fashion that best suits our needs, to the God or gods of our choice—or to no god at all. There is nothing to fight about if we allow that everyone has a valid opinion.

A woman I know stopped arguing years ago with her father. Whenever he heats up for a confrontation, she walks away. She learned while still in her teens that he had the overwhelming need to be right. Sometimes he is, and sometimes he isn't. It makes no difference in the long run. However, on those occasions when he is proven wrong, he chokes on the slice of humble pie he must eat.

So here's the lesson for this day: The case is never closed. There is always room for another opinion. And whether you are right or not doesn't matter. If your ego needs stroking so badly, give yourself a positive affirmation instead of bashing someone else's thought process.

Do You Have an NBA?

No, NBA is not the National Basketball Association. My new acronym stands for Negative Belief Attitude.

If you have an NBA, you are probably waiting for something bad to happen. When it does, you proudly exclaim: "I knew it!"

You, my friend, are stuck in the proverbial self-fulfilling prophecy syndrome.

NBAs are not earned in college but in the school of hard knocks known as life. Unlike school, where we are stuck with the grades given by our teachers, in the school of life we can change our grades as we desire.

NBAs are deadly. Aren't you tired of saying or hearing:

- I don't have enough time, money, clothes.
- My wife, husband, friends don't back me up.
- My spouse, boss, parents abuse me.
- Nobody listens, believes me, loves me.
- I can't do anything right.

As Ann Landers would say, "kwitcherbeefing." Get positive.

If your life scores are barely passing, think of success as a ladder (the ladder of success, get it?). Take one step at a time. Start with self-actualizing. Set the goal then add self-esteem, self-approval, selfconfidence. Don't look down. That's where the NBAs are waiting to get you.

A nonjudgmental attitude will help in your quest for knowledge, understanding and further exploration.

As you reach the top, add aesthetics—symmetry, order and beauty—so that you will graduate with self-fulfillment of your human potential and a PBA.

Now that you're a graduate, I don't need to spell that one out for you. That's right. You got it.

Excuses

Examine each of your favorite excuses closely. Think carefully about them, then paraphrase. I'll bet they all come out sounding something like this: "I'm no good," or "I'm not good enough... ."

How many of you reading this really believe that you're not good enough?

Even one is too many.

Behavioral psychologists say about *80 percent* of the population, even those leading successful lives, believe deep down inside that they are failures because of one shortcoming or another.

On four separate occasions I have had individuals who are well-off tell me how utterly worthless they felt. Two of these men own their own business, one is a nutritionist, and the last is a public speaker. None of these men know each other, yet each of them expressed the same negative sentiment.

If, as philosophers say, *we become what we think about,* then let us all try to think that we are prosperous and important. Let us acknowledge that each of us has a purpose here on Earth to make life a bit more enjoyable. Let us do away with justifications and rationalizations.

No excuses. Case closed!

Rewards of Reading

Regardless of their earnings, Americans spend almost *10 times* as much on entertainment as they do on books. This statistic astounds me. It also sets me to thinking about our woeful educational system.

Here are two interesting quotes on the subject:

- "Education is what survives when what has been learned has been forgotten."—B. F. Skinner.
- "Nothing in education is so astonishing as the amount of ignorance it accumulates in the form of inert facts."—Henry Adams.

Although times have changed, not much has advanced in the field of education.

The dictionary's definition of educate is "to develop mentally, morally or aesthetically." Yet teachers are burning out trying to cram useless facts and figures into the minds of their students. Sadly, they are not listening. Instead they are dreaming of being rock stars instead of rocket scientists, millionaires instead of marketing managers, comedians instead of CEOs.

How do we get the point across that, in order to get ahead, students must be encouraged to read? Parents must show them that stretching their imagination is the only way to succeed. Think about it. If your child spent as many hours reading as he or she does talking on the phone or watching television, you'd have a budding genius.

Do you set a good example or do you turn on the television when you walk in the door and stay there until it's time for bed?

Children see parents as a higher self, an extension of where they will be a generation from now. If you're a couch potato with no ambition, chances are that's how your kid will end up.

Ever notice how many doctors had fathers who were doctors, ditto for dentists, actors, attorneys?

If you are spending 10 times more on entertainment than books, please make sure the entertainment has an educational value. Forget the videos and visit a museum, ditch the CDs and go to the planetarium, buy a telescope instead of a new television.

Set you and your offspring on the quest for higher learning and you will be pleasantly rewarded at the output of higher potential.

"All religions must be tolerated… for… every man must get to heaven his own way."

FREDERICK THE GREAT

"Always do right. This will gratify some people and astonish the rest."

MARK TWAIN

"A child miseducated is a child lost."

JOHN F. KENNEDY

E Is for Einstein

"Small is the number of them that see with their own eyes and feel with their own hearts," said Albert Einstein.

The operant word here is "own."

He understood that most of us are products of outside conditioning and see the world from an external viewpoint. We *feel* based on the input we receive from those around us.

Seeing with our own eyes and feeling with our own hearts would mean a return to our original innocence. If we can get past what our senses bring into our lives, we would find a world filled with intuition, insight, innate intelligence and inspiration.

Einstein was an *original* thinker who believed that *originality* was more important than rote knowledge (why do you think his teachers wanted him kicked out of school?). He took basic information, subjected it to his formidable ingenuity, and turned it into new and innovative concepts.

Another of his favorite sayings was: "God does not play with dice."

Einstein understood that the world is an orderly place with time and space working together for the ultimate good. He believed in contributing to this natural order of things, not depleting it. In spite of his accomplishments he remained a humble person, grateful for his intellectual gifts.

We can all take a lesson from this great man. He is an example of positive energy and what a person can donate to mankind.

Memories

When my family arrived from Casablanca, Morocco, in April 1943, we entered the United States via Ellis Island. For months, I walked the streets of New York, ducking whenever I saw a uniformed policeman. He reminded me of the Nazi officers who visited Casablanca. It took a long time before I understood who the good guys were and that I had nothing to fear.

My mother had the curious habit of stapling the tags that came on pillows and chairs so they wouldn't come off by accident. The labels which read "Do not remove under penalty of law" were a constant reminder of the terrible regime we had narrowly escaped.

We may laugh at this now, but how many of us act irrationally when it comes to the law or religious restrictions? As the Nazis showed so well, control by fear is the best way to conquer the spirit of man.

I could go off here on a dissertation of control and fear but I'll save that for another day. The topic for today is memories.

If remembrances are painful, use them to serve as a way of making today better than yesterday. I choose to learn from my past experiences but I will not suffer over them. History is history. Let it go.

P.S. My mother no longer staples the labels on. In fact, she delights in tearing them off and throwing them away. She's a fast learner.

Aspirin

I rarely get headaches. So I took two aspirins a few nights ago—at least I thought they were aspirin. When I mentioned it to my wife in the morning she told me that I had actually taken two of her antibiotics which she was keeping in a Nuprin bottle.

Because I believed they were aspirin, I felt better. That's the power of placebos—and also the power of the mind.

The mind controls the body, an ancient notion that has been proved throughout the centuries. Recently scientific studies published in a book *Placebo Theory, Research and Mechanics* show that placebos release substances within the brain which act as pain killers and which can activate the body's immunological system.

You have heard the phrase, the mind is a terrible thing to waste. That is true.

Nobel Prize winner John Steinbeck wrote: "It is the nature of man to rise to greatness, if greatness is *expected* of him."

If we pay attention to life, we will learn a myriad of lessons. Pay is the key word. If we don't pay attention, we pay in other ways.

I believe that headaches are caused by infectious negativity. Likewise, optimism is a powerful opiate. Use it as often as needed. You cannot overdose on it, and your headaches will go the way of the dinosaurs.

Lost Instructions

Most new toys, games, gadgets and tools come with instructions. Unfortunately, life does not come with a training manual. We learn as we go, by trial and error.

There are, however, several basic tenets which we can use as an outline for the chapters of our existence. They go like this:

1. I am made in the image of God.
2. My main source of nourishment is love.
3. I have intuitive knowledge of the world.
4. I have unlimited human potential.

Instead of following these guidelines, parents write their own directions based on their neurotic needs. Those neuroses are passed down from generation to generation, with new ones being added all the time.

Parents should be required to take a written and oral exam designed to ensure that they can follow the simple instructions outlined above when raising their children. This thought is even more essential nowadays with teen pregnancies and the proliferation of drug and alcohol abuse. Too many prospective mothers and fathers wallow in their own lack of self-esteem to pass any positive values onto their offspring. This sad state of affairs will continue to repeat itself. It is repeating itself right now as social standards slip far below what is acceptable, even in this open-minded era.

Parenting is the most difficult job anybody can undertake. Tradespeople require licenses to prove their expertise. Moms and dads need nothing. If the national Parent Teacher Association is right, parents give their children *eight negative strokes* for each positive stroke.

Those statistics are chilling and sad. Is it any wonder that crime is rampant, committed by younger and younger tykes.

A little girl stabs her playmate over a Barbie doll. Two pre-teen boys wire a bomb into their classroom to blow up their teacher. Friends shoot each other with guns found in dresser drawers. The list is endless.

Teach your children about God, love, intuitive knowledge and unlimited human potential. Believe it yourself and those timeless values will bring immeasurable rewards.

Fireflies

Don't you think this is an appropriate title for a hot July night? Fireflies light up the world in their own special way. They have just one way of doing this, by illuminating their abdomen with a flashing light.

Humans, on the other hand, have many ways to shine.

At birth we are given an average of nearly 500 thousand hours in which to be productive (assuming you live to age 75). If you plan to use nearly 100 thousand, or one-fifth, of that allotted time in a job, shouldn't you be something you *like?*

Ask yourself these questions about your present employment:

- Why did I choose this line of work?
- Am I happy doing this?
- What would I want to be if I could be anything?

Changing jobs is not difficult if the mind is programmed. Then you are moving *toward* something you want, not *away* from a contrary place. If you want the new more than the old, set up a healthy mental state which can move you down the road to your new-found happiness.

Let's say that you're not sure it will work out, then try it part-time or on a limited basis until you know for certain.

A lady who had a steady job, but one which she was overqualified for, kept her eye open for a better opportunity. When it came along, she became nervous. What if she didn't like her new employer, what if she couldn't handle the assigned duties, what if they didn't like her? She didn't want to leave the old job and give up her benefits for a position she was not sure about.

To test the waters, she took off from work and tried the new job for a day. Voila`. Everyone got along. The skills she had acquired over the years suited the employers and she found she could handle the responsibilities.

She gave notice the following day and began preparing herself mentally for the increased paycheck she will be getting.

Taking *calculated* risks is part of life. There are many ways to shine like a firefly. But first you have to fly—by the seat of your pants if you must. Just like the firefly takes a chance of being caught when it lights up, you, too, must take chances in order to succeed.

*"What you do not want done to yourself,
do not do to others!"*

CONFUCIUS

*"It's what you learn after you know it all
that counts."*

JOHN WOODEN

*"You'll never really know what I mean and I'll
never know exactly what you mean."*

MIKE NICHOLS

Repent Now

Ever see the Ziggy cartoons with the bum holding a "Repent Now" sign?

Contrary to popular belief, the word repent does not always pertain to sinning—it can be used for simply changing one's mind.

When a mental adjustment is made, an attitude adjustment is not far behind. This is seen dramatically with terminally ill patients. Those who give up, die. Those who decide to fight for their lives often prolong the inevitable and, in some cases, miraculously reverse the disease altogether.

Years ago I worked with a woman who was easily the greatest man-hating cynic I ever encountered. Sally had been abused and abandoned. She vowed to steer clear of the male species altogether. She lived for her children, a single mother who thought life was a bummer, and vowed that no man would ever fill a permanent niche in her home.

I phoned Sally not long ago for some information and thought at first I had dialed the wrong number. Her enthusiasm nearly bowled me over, her laughter tinkled like a crystal chandelier. Sally positively sparkled over the phone. I decided I had to see her in person.

A week later I arrived at her place of business, a store specializing in futon couches, where Sally and her new husband worked in harmony. As we chatted, she revealed that a friend convinced her that the negativity she was dishing out was only coming back to her. If she wanted to change her life, she had to change her vibes.

Sally "repented" and less than three weeks later she met a new guy. They married after a short engagement while on a futon convention in Virginia.

I am convinced these two will have a "happy ever after" life. One just has to see the twinkle in their eyes and the happy laughter to know she has truly broken the bonds of the past and is looking forward to a wonderful life as a wife.

Early Birds

They say the early bird gets the worm, but I'm not sure about that after a recent incident.

I called a local high school where I was giving a lecture and asked to speak to Mrs. X. I was told she had left for the day.

"Doesn't she work until three?" I asked.

"Yes," was the reply.

"But it's only a quarter to three," I protested.

"She leaves early," said the secretary.

Now that's a sweet deal. Add up the amount of time this woman is cheating the school board out of, at the taxpayers' expense. That's my money and yours she is spending by skipping out early every day.

Doing a job well has a built-in satisfaction meter. It frees us mentally and emotionally so we can enjoy our time off because we *earned* it.

The immigrants who came here during the early 1900s did not even speak the language. Yet they toiled 14—and 16-hour days just to make ends meet. Even children were not exempt from hard days and nights of back-breaking labor.

Today a standard joke goes like this: "When did he first start working for you?" The answer: "When I threatened to fire him."

While many of us get our bodies to work and keep them in our chairs until quitting time, how many of the hours spent are truly productive? There are chats at the coffee pot and water cooler, the trips to the john or out for a smoke, there are two and even three-hour lunches. And if everyone leaves 15 minutes early like Mrs. X, it is no wonder the economy is sagging.

Work separates humanity from other living creatures. Perhaps we should take some lessons from the ants and the bees. I know Mrs. X could use a refresher course in work ethics. Be sure you're part of the solution, not the problem.

The Circus

The circus is coming to town. When I was young I loved the bit with the little red car which drives into center ring. Then out climbs an endless procession of people—men and women in colorful costumes.

As a grownup I see an analogy with the three rings under the circus tent. I've labeled them Physical, Mental and Spiritual.

The Physical ring represents our bodies which we must maintain in a healthy way so it can provide a nurturing environment for our Mental and Spiritual sides.

The Mental ring is our logical thought process. We can have positive expectancy even though circumstances are adverse. Likewise, we can have negative attitudes even when everything is going just fine.

The Spiritual ring is our unlimited potential for growth and our intuitive intelligence. This is where our "gut" level resides, the part of us that keeps us free from danger if we listen to it.

In this circus of life, the key to happiness is uniting the three rings into one cohesive and optimistic whole.

Then, instead of 20 different fools getting out of the car, it will be just one well-adjusted individual. You.

The Best

My definition of the best is to be the best one can be—not the best there is. Let me clarify that.

For years I went out of my way to a restaurant that served mediocre food. Once seated in my favorite booth, I forgot about the long ride and bland cooking when my friend Alice came over with a big friendly smile carrying the menu.

Alice was well into her sixties but she could run rings around the younger waitresses. She always recommended the pancakes, with the fruit in season, since that was the best thing on the menu. The emotional perks I received from her were far more nourishing than the food. *Alice was the best she could be.*

I once asked Alice to be on the weekly television show I hosted called "Positive Living." She refused. She was afraid to divulge her age since she figured her employer would fire her for being too old to do her job (even though she did it perfectly).

The restaurant is now out of business and Alice has disappeared from my life. Even a superb waitress cannot keep a restaurant going if the food is lousy. Hopefully Alice has found other employment and is still dishing out her good cheer.

I have found another "best" at the local gas station. He's a kindly old gent with a kind word and a grin whenever I stop by to refuel. Of all the gas station attendants I've encountered, he's the only one who gives a little extra something to the customers.

Do you personify the best? Are you being the best worker, the best boss, the best spouse, the best parent you can be?

Write down your definition of the word and see how it compares to mine. Being the best does not mean you have to be the smartest in your class, or the fastest on the track, or the salesman who sells the most.

Being the best is being all you can be—that's all anyone can ask of you and that's all you can ask of yourself.

Join the PGA

I am thinking of joining the PGA. That's not the Professional Golf Association. It's my own organization called the Personal Growth Alliance.

In my PGA there would be no competition against others. You would only compete against yourself, striving to better your past performance. I guarantee true growth and no bad feelings.

My motto will be "I left the world a little better than I found it." Golfers can't make that claim even if they shoot ten under par.

Becoming a member of my PGA requires a commitment to selfimprovement. This can be done with seminars, books, tapes, videos and any other method you want to use to enhance your self-knowledge and self-image.

Everybody would have an "enthusiasm" card. We would have weekly discussions about the eminent thinkers and the classics. We would listen to masterpieces by famous composers and visit museums where the great works of art are hung.

We would strive to lead *expressive lives* and minimize negativity. We would be risk-takers, not victims, who participate instead of sitting on the sidelines while others tee off.

My PGA would be open to anyone who wants to join. For more information, please give me a call. Or, even better, start your own Personal Growth Alliance with your family, friends and peers. Be the leader, encourage well-being and discourage competition.

Give pats on the back and words of praise. They work as well as a hole-in-one.

*Three bear hunters approached the park entrance.
Posted at the gate was a sign that read Bear Left.
The hunters turned around and went home.
Do you take everything so literally?*

Miscommunication

During my travels I have made it a hobby to collect signs with incorrect translations. They always generate a chuckle.

- In a Japanese hotel: You are invited to take advantage of the chambermaid.
- In a Norwegian tavern: Ladies are requested not to have children at the bar.
- In a Hong Kong supermarket: For your convenience we recommend courteous, efficient *self-service.*
- At a Swiss hotel: Because of the impropriety of entertaining guests of the opposite sex in the bedroom, we suggest you use the lobby for this purpose.

Communication is the key to understanding. When we input information into a computer, the feedback is the same as what we have put in. But when we feed data into another human, it invariably gets garbled.

Remember the old game of telephone? One person whispered a phrase to another and that phrase was repeated again and again, as it passed around the circle. The final result always produces hysterical results, but it never bears any resemblance to the original.

One of the most effective tools to clear communication is to repeat back what you have been told. If your boss or spouse gives you a directive, say: "You want me to… ." then repeat exactly what you heard. You'll be surprised how many mistakes are cleared up before they are made and how easy it is to follow directions when you are in sync with the person giving the orders.

Here are some gems on the subject of communication:

- E. B. White: "Be obscure clearly."
- Ralph Waldo Emerson: "It is a luxury to be understood."
- William James: "The most immutable barrier in nature is between one man's thoughts and another's."
- JohnW. Roper: "To say the right thing at the right time, keep still most of the time."
- T. S. Matthews: "Communication is something so simple and difficult that we can never put it in simple words."

Action v. Inaction

I was taking my usual daily walk carrying two five-pound weights when I encountered a young man with a beer gut. We nodded and said "Good morning." As he passed he muttered: "That's what *I* should be doing."

I went on my merry way thinking that this is something he probably will never be doing. For we rarely turn a "should" into action.

Let me give you some hints at how you can get started if you want to change your life around.

First make a list of all the goals you would like to attain.

Next make a list of all the things holding you back—the problems and obstacles that you believe stand in the way of your success.

Now take the second list and tear it in half, and in half again, and again until you have a mound of tiny scraps.

Why would I ask you to do this? I'm asking you to shred your *excuses*. You have the power to remove the barriers to achievement. You have to work at it until those hurdles are no more significant than those scraps in the garbage.

Don't worry if you feel silly doing it, or if it seems meaningless to you. Just *do it*. The action will reinforce what you've been reading and help imprint a new positive attitude in your mind.

Turn the Other Cheek

When Terry Anderson was released by his captors after six-and-ahalf years as a hostage in Beirut, he *forgave* his tormentors. He would have had every right to plot revenge, but he decided to take a Christian stance and turn the other cheek.

Anderson's actions stand like a beacon for truth and ethical behavior. He can be held aloft as a role model of the highest order.

E. H. Chapin, who lived from 1814 to 1889, said: "Never does the human soul appear so strong as when it forgoes revenge, and dares forgive an injury."

He would have been proud of Anderson.

We can only wonder what was going through Anderson's mind while he was in captivity. He must have repeated over again "Where there's life there's hope."

As a refugee from Europe during the Nazi regime, I admire Anderson's ability to forgive. It took me decades to get over my hurt and anger. Even now I cannot begin to love my former enemy.

Anderson embodies the essence of what it means to truly live one's life based on a deep religious belief—one that transcends today's conditional morality.

Overcoming Obstacles

Time Is Short

Today the average person knows many more people than the average citizen did a century ago. Telecommunications and electronic networking allow us to reach out and touch thousands of others instead of being limited to a narrow circle of friends, relatives and peers.

Sadly, with this huge collection of associates, individuals become disposable instead of indispensable. Old friends are no longer treated like gold, they are too easily forgotten, especially if there has been a disagreement. Ditto for families. How many relatives are you on the outs with?

In 1879, Phillips Brooks, a Boston bishop, delivered a sermon to his congregation in Trinity Church. His words have generated some famous quotes:

"You, who are letting your friend's heart ache for a word of appreciation or sympathy, the time is short."

And this: "*Don't wait* to patch up that quarrel. *Don't wait* to say that kind work, to do that kind deed."

How about this: "The time is short and tomorrow may be too late."

A young woman I know meant to call her sister who lived in another state. Each day she put it off, thinking that she would do it tomorrow. Then one evening her father called and told her that her sister had died that day from a stroke. It was too late. The young woman still feels guilty that she did not take the time to pick up the phone.

Get into the habit of doing things *today*. Time *is* short and a kind word, a moment of appreciation, or sympathetic chat can make somebody's day turn from gloomy to bright. And we never know if it will be their last day or ours.

Rewards for kind acts come back to each of us like a boomerang. Try it today and see if it works. *Put the book down* and pick up the telephone. Call someone you have not spoken to for a long time or touch base with a friend or family member you've been meaning to call.

It is guaranteed to enhance your good feelings and erase guilt. See you tomorrow.

Letting Go

Take a balloon filled with helium and attach a cement cube to its string. When you cut the string the balloon will soar into the atmosphere, fulfilling its destiny.

The same holds true of people. The cement cube represents old guilts and angers firmly anchored in our subconscious. These cubes cause us to stay well below our potential level of accomplishment. In order to soar we must cut the cords that bind us to our past.

We must learn to forgive our enemies and those who caused us harm. We must learn to become the best we can be.

Think of yourself as water, which is the best example of nonresistance. Water will glide and flow over and under. It surrounds, fills, gushes and trickles, depending on circumstances. It is completely adaptable. Water can swirl or remain calm as glass. It can turn to ice or boil itself away.

To put it simply, be like water—go with the flow.

"Repartee: What a person thinks of after he becomes a departee."

DAN BENNETT

"An optimist proclaims that we live in the best of all possible worlds, and the pessimist fears this is true."

JAMES BRANCH

Problems

This is a conversation between God and Adam, the original man.

"Adam, you don't look very happy," said God. "You've got everything you could possibly want—you live in paradise. What's wrong?"

"You're right," said Adam. "This is paradise and that's the problem. I have nothing to do, nobody to talk to. Even the animals have mates."

"What do you have in mind?"

"I could use someone to pick the fruit for me and wash the vegetables. How about someone to scratch my back?"

"If you're talking about a slave, I can get you one. But it will cost an arm and a leg," said God.

"But God, my arms and legs balance my body. How about using a rib? I have many of those."

And that's how Adam got Eve and kept his sense of balance.

Today we find that the most balanced people are those who live as couples. Love is the way to find heaven on Earth. Research has shown that people live longer when they are in stable monogamous relationships.

Katharine Hepburn, a known cynic when it comes to marriage, once said this: "If you want to sacrifice the admiration of many men for the criticism of one, go ahead, get married."

I believe by remaining single, she missed out on the joys of wedded bliss.

What we must beware of when we join with another is not to adopt Adam's attitude. Marriage is a two-wa street, neither party should make a slave of the other. Respect for the feelings of both husband and wife must be taken into consideration whenever a decision is made. On a day-to-day basis, treating your partner with regard should be a top priority.

No top dogs allowed in paradise.

The Great Family Hoax

Family: a group of peoples regarded as deriving from common stock.

If we trace our origins back to the primates—to the family of anthropoids—we must admit that we are in the same extended family as everyone else in the world, regardless of race or religion.

Yet we grow up in most cases with a *"them or us"* attitude. Even worse, many have adopted the mentality of us *versus* them. The youth gangs these days are the worst personification of this problem. They feel justified in shooting a "brother" because he wears a baseball cap with an emblem of a different team.

When a New York teenager was asked why he stabbed a complete stranger to death, he replied: "I didn't like his accent."

Where are this boy's parents and what are they teaching him?

The minute a child is taught that he or she is better or superior to another, hate begins. This dysfunctional way of living cloaks the individual with a mantle of intellectual darkness which may never be eliminated. To kill over a cap or a different ideology makes no sense.

Intolerance and prejudice eclipse a world of love and reverence. If we were truly one functional family of man, there would be no separation due to color, race or religion.

I say the family of man is a hoax that can only be laid to rest by teaching our children that we are all made in God's image, whether we have dark skin or light, whether our hair is curly or straight, whether our eyes are blue, brown or slanted. Being color blind can be a blessing in disguise.

Tele-Manners

As you know by now, my son is 15—a budding teen with lots of female callers. To improve our communications, I started asking his girlfriends to identify themselves when they called. Guess what? They hung up on me!

I like his young friends and I'm sorry they now see me as a nosy old ogre. But it makes me wonder what they are learning at home. Are their parents teaching them the basic etiquette for interacting in society? Apparently not.

Even though I have become a pariah at home (for my now ex-wife agrees with my son that I should not ask who is calling), I firmly believe that identifying oneself when calling is important. Politeness goes a long way.

When telemarketers and solicitors call, and they always seem to pick dinner time to do their work, I have to bite my tongue not to bark into the receiver to leave me alone. I calm myself down because I know they are just doing their job. It's a lot better than being on welfare. When irate customers scream at them or slam the phone down, they are perpetuating a negative attitude. The telemarketer has a few dozen people do this in any given shift and what do you think he does? He takes it out on his co-workers and his family. It's a vicious cycle.

In the real world, most business is done via the phone. The people with the positive attitudes and innate politeness go furthest when face to—face meetings cannot be arranged.

Take a look at your own telephone manners. Are they up to par? Have you taught your children well? I may be an old fuddy-duddy in some respects, but I know a thing or two. I hope I've rung a bell with this thought.

Affirmations

Here are some affirmations:

- I am incapable.
- I hate myself.
- I'm stupid.
- I knew I would mess up.

Surprised you, didn't I? You thought affirmations were only positive things you say to yourself. Affirmations are simply affirmations. They can be positive or negative. They solidify any thought or idea you have. And they work—to your *disadvantage* or *advantage*.

In the Bible it is written, "What you think and feel so you will become." In today's lingo, "What you affirm is how you will live."

The beauty of affirmations is that you can control them once you are aware of what you are doing. The power to choose is yours. And look at the difference:

- I am capable.
- I love myself.
- I'm smart.
- I knew I could do it.

Choose peace of mind, harmony, success, love, and affirm daily until it becomes second nature and you are living a life of positives. Negatives belong in a photographer's studio, not in your mind.

No Free Lunch

"There's no free lunch."

"The buck stops here."

I taught those two phrases to the four-year-old son of a woman I was dating. Most people thought it was cute when he said it and thought they could stump him when they asked him what it meant. But he had all the answers.

"There's no free lunch means you have to pay for everything," he'd say. "The buck stops here means I am responsible for everything I do."

If four-year-olds can repeat and explain these simple concepts, why can't grown-ups live by them?

Sadly, America has one of the highest divorce rates; we lead the world in homicides; we lock up more people than in any other country. Our moral and ethical behavior is in the gutter.

If we want to turn things around we must learn that nothing is free and we are responsible for our actions. This universe operates on the laws of cause and effect.

Lack of morals and ethics will come back to haunt us again and again. Moral strength begins with self-knowledge which is tied to healthy self-esteem—gained through kindness, grace, and empathy for others. For those individuals who are left to grow up without a compassionate word, self-esteem must be achieved in spite of the void.

I was reading about a young killer who died in the electric chair. His supporters wanted clemency citing his harsh, abusive upbringing. They said two of his brothers also spent time in jail. One of them died violently. We should have empathy and give him a break. The flip side of the coin was that the killer also had a brother and sister who, in spite of their adverse childhood, managed to put their sordid past behind them and become productive members of society.

Everything you do or say has a price to pay. Whether or not you believe in the boomerang theory, goodness is repaid with goodness, and vice versa. Likewise, *you* are responsible for all your actions. The dog didn't eat your homework, you just didn't do it.

There's no free lunch and the buck stops here. Have a nice weekend!

"Tolerance is the virtue of the man without convictions."

G. K. CHESTERTON

"If at first you don't succeed, you're running about average."

M. H. ALDERSON

Expectations

Not long ago I had a meeting with a prospective client. We agreed to meet at a local restaurant since we not know what the other looked like. I arrived on time and waited outside. Twenty minutes later, wondering whether I was being "stood up," a waitress poked her head out of the door and asked if I was waiting for Mr. G. He had arrived a few minutes before I did and took a booth inside.

We both had expectations. He expected me to wander inside. I expected him to wait outside. What are your expectations?

Assumptions can be wonderful, and they can be dangerous.

Remember the classic episode of *The Odd Couple* in which Felix and Oscar have an argument over some tickets? Felix turns to Oscar and says in his whining voice: "When you assume, you make an 'ass' out of 'u' and 'me.'"

Expecting to achieve unrealistic goals will lead to despair and unhappiness. The first time you put on jogging shoes don't expect to run a marathon. Don't even expect to run a mile. Perhaps you'll go a block or two before you're winded. Take it a little at a time, adding an additional block each day, building up your endurance.

Without expectations, life can be quite bleak. We all need goals in order to push us to better ourselves—to make more money, to achieve higher grades, to produce a better sales record.

My expectation is to write one of these vignettes per day. When I am at home I can stay on track. My expectations are realistic. However, when I am traveling, lecturing and sleeping in strange hotels, I fall behind in my schedule. Instead of getting down on myself, I vow to make it up when I get home. I try to keep my expectations on a realistic plane so I won't become discouraged and give up the project.

Learn to temper your expectations, not only of yourself but of those around you, to reasonable limits. If your child brings home B grades, there is no need to rant or rave about getting A's. Chances are your kid is already beating up on him or herself to do better. Perhaps that's the best he or she can do. Let your child set expectations that are commensurate with his or her abilities. Do the same for yourself.

Dead Poet's Society

Have you seen the movie *Dead Poet's Society* with Robin Williams as the inspirational teacher? I saw it on television and every time the picture hit an emotional high, the screen went blank and a slew of moronic commercials filled the room. It made me want to cry for the young poets who will never be properly stimulated because of the desensitizing "words from our sponsor."

We are living in an illusory world where fact and fiction merge making it difficult for old and young alike to sort the real from the unreal. Look at the whole Dan Quayle-Murphy Brown incident. Even the vice president of America could not separate a television sitcom from actual life.

I have worked with school children and I know they are confused and frustrated. They want the truth, but it continues to elude them. Eventually, reinforced fiction becomes truth. The new morality has more shades of gray than a battleship.

The self-image of these kids will improve only to the degree that they receive and accept time-honored values that are not open to subjective interpretation—like honesty, truth, respect.

Several years ago the national Parent-Teacher Association declared that the first priority of the schools should be the enrichment of a child's self-esteem. It would be wonderful if that could become a reality and there would be no need for emotionally starved youngsters to band together into a dead poet's society.

Altus

Altus is the mythical bird in Greek lore which flew higher and deeper than all the rest. It is the logo on my recently released tapes. Altus symbolizes my philosophy: We should be the best we can be—both to the outside world as well as the world within each of us.

"You cannot change the wind but you can alter your wings," is one of the sayings on my tape. We cannot control external events. However we can control *our reactions* to them. This requires a process called thinking, and there's the rub.

New data indicates that from a total of 40 hours per week, the average American spends one hour thinking! Nearly 20 hours are lost to mindless entertainment which prevents us from using our minds at all.

If we become what we think, the future is bleak. Fifty years ago Nobel prize winner Dr. Albert Schweitzer was asked what he believed was wrong with people.

"They just don't think," he answered without hesitation.

Perhaps we should rephrase the old adage "An apple a day keeps the doctor away," to "A thought a day keeps the couch potatoes awake."

UFO

Unidentified Flying Object may be what UFO stands for in scientific terms. To me it stands for the best method of handling human problems. Since our ego continually interferes when we relate to others, I suggest that my acronym UFO stands for Understanding, Forgiveness and Optimism.

Understanding why people act as they do and accepting them is the first step in personal growth and development.

Forgiveness can relieve both physical and mental illness in both the (for)giver and the recipient (forgiven). (Talk about a negative title for a film: *The Unforgiven*!) Pardoning a transgression gets rid of guilt, anger, frustration and hatred.

Optimism keeps the opportunity to improve relationships on the front burner instead of the back one. When a problem is unresolved I often feel like I am living in suspended animation (like an alien UFO). I much prefer to stay on top of things, keeping an open eye for ways to improve one-on-one associations at home, at work and with my friends.

Psychologists find that most people sit around waiting for something to happen. I say, put your ego in your back pocket and take charge of your life. I guarantee it's worth the effort.

Success or Failure?

According to statistics, four out of five people have a strong fear of failing. In addition, more than 70 percent of high achievers feel they are imposters in spite of their obvious success.

To fear failure is understandable. Most people with low self-images will not attempt new career changes. Their feelings of inferiority hold them back and reinforce their mediocrity. They become known in the trade as "don't-rock-the-boat" philosophers. They include many bluecollar workers with menial jobs who do not take chances and won't move off the assembly line.

The high achievers who suffer from the "imposter phenomenon" feel better about themselves. However, when they reach a new level of accomplishment they feel they are undeserving of praise and financial reward. They claim luck, or being in the right place and time, contributed to their advancement. They rarely give credit to their own innate talents.

Past negative conditioning is the culprit in both cases. When inner security is affected, guilt and lack of self-worth creeps in, eroding our foundation.

For those of us who fear failure or feel undeserving of promotion, we must review the past and the victories of our childhood. It doesn't have to be winning a foot race or a prize at the science fair. Small victories of any kind add to the positive attitude we need to succeed.

A friend won third prize in a drawing contest in seventh grade. That small victory stayed with her for years, giving her inner strength to pursue a career as an artist.

Forget the times you lost or got a failing grade for your efforts. Think positive and it will carry you to new heights.

"Change your thoughts and you change your world."

NORMAN VINCENT PEALE

"When all men think alike, no one thinks very much."

WALTER LIPPMANN

"People are always blaming their circumstances for what they are."

GEORGE BERNARD SHAW

Humane Relations

Recently, while I was being taped for a radio show, the producer asked me some interesting questions:

- Why is it that almost everything you say and do is already known by the bulk of your audiences?
- Why can't they use that information without waiting for you to motivate them?

My answers were not difficult. It's like driving a nail into a block of wood. Repetition will hammer the point home.

If we feel we don't deserve to live a healthier, happier life, nothing anybody can do will force a change for the better. It's a funny thing about life, it usually gives you *exactly* what you *subconsciously demand* of it. Therefore, if change is what you want, you must first alter your mind and your attitude. You can make it a conscious decision and through constant repetition it will filter down until it becomes a new habit or thought.

There's no doubt about it, life is worth living. If you don't know that by now, keep reading. Hopefully by the last page you will have learned your lessons well. If not, start again or pick up this book whenever you feel you need a mental boost.

The Full Life

"Get your bloated nothingness out of the way," said Ralph Waldo Emerson.

That blunt advice is important for today's high stress times. Emerson believed in living the full life and not cheating one's way out of it.

Here's my acronym for a FULL life:

Forgive others. Forget fear forever.
Understand and accept the *uniqueness* of others.
Love and accept love liberally.
Live and *let live. Laugh* whenever possible.

Since life gives back what you invest in it, your moves will determine the level of living you do. The more you accept, the more acceptance you will receive. When you praise others, you raise their self esteem and your own.

Likewise, criticize and you will attract criticism. Be envious and your mind is not receptive.

Peace of mind and flexibility are what comes to mind when I think of a person who has his or her act together. Having an adaptable philosophy, which allows other opinions to coexist with yours, is a valuable mental asset.

Most people grow best when they interact with others showing patience, compassion, empathy and altruism. The trick is to broaden your people skills by using them at every opportunity.

Image

I recently had an experience I shall quickly put behind me. I bought a new telephone which did not work. When I brought it back to the store I found a similar model for the same price and asked for an even exchange. The young woman behind the counter did not smile, she did not acknowledge my presence and, in fact she did not say one word to me except "Sign this" as she pushed the receipt and a pen toward me.

Truthfully, I feel sorry for her. What a miserable life she must be leading when a smile or a nod is too much to ask. I was polite, not a word about what lousy products are made these days. All I said was "I'd like to exchange this."

So there is a lesson here and it's this. Think about the image you project to others. Are you cynical, negative, curt, irritable or downright nasty? If so, you need an immediate attitude adjustment. Get a grip on your attitude.

The woman's job, for which she gets paid an honest wage (even if it is a low one), is to be helpful, not rude. Customers who leave her counter feeling negative will carry those bad vibrations around with them, spewing them onto others. Not me. I left her spoiled rotten spirit when I passed through the store doors into the parking lot. I refused to let her ruin my day.

Foot-in-Mouth Disease

I love fortune cookies, even though the message inside doesn't always make sense to me. My most recent one read: He who has learning without imagination has feet but no wings.

That's exactly what I am seeing in the business world today. Managers, supervisors and salespeople seem to know their jobs but their interpersonal relations lag way behind. It reminds me of attorneys who spend so much time reading their law books that they don't know how to deal with their clients.

A lawyer, recommended by a friend to represent me during the sale of my home nearly blew the deal because he could not communicate effectively with the buyers. The nuns who taught us in Brussels suggested we roll our tongues around our mouths seven times before we spoke. That gives the brain time to kick in and censor itself. It's not the worst idea, even if it is time-consuming.

I prefer this analogy: The drive gear of your car will always propel you forward, reverse will always back you up. If we translate that into positive and negative, remember to put your mental car in forward gear and keep it there.

"Man, unlike any other thing organic or inorganic in the universe, grows beyond his work, walks up the stairs of his concepts, emerges ahead of his accomplishments," wrote John Steinbeck in *The Grapes of Wrath*.

As an old Arab saying goes: "He is the master of his unspoken words and slave to those that he has uttered."

The Natural

Most of us don't have the luxury the BionicMan did. Our parts wear out and, although science can make them better for a while, they eventually break down altogether.

I have dozens of books on holistic healing and we have the ability within ourselves to keep our bodies healthy, one cell at a time. We also have the talent for breaking down the cells so they die before their allotted time.

God gives us a body and mind filled with potential. Unfortunately, too many of us interfere with the natural order of things. This leads to a mediocre or average life at best.

I believe the problem started when we began using our egos to think that we were in charge. Here are a few examples of thinking versus feeling:

- We'd rather win than heal.
- We'd rather cry than laugh.
- We'd rather judge than accept.
- We'd rather be right than be happy.
- We prefer being fearful to being loving.
- We'd rather suffer than have peace of mind.

Why would we choose this self-destructive pattern when all the philosophical and religious works tell us we can be happy, loving and giving?

I must repeat it once again even though you may be tired of hearing it: We are filled with guilt from the past and feel we are unworthy.

Doctors may fix your broken bones and worn-out knees; they can give you a new heart and unclog your arteries. They can pull your face so tight you look like a teenager. But only you can clean the debris from your mind.

*"Creative minds always have been known to
survive any kind of bad training."*

ANNA FREUD

"The past is but the beginning of a beginning."

H. G. WELLS

*"Nothing contributes so much in tranquilizing the
mind as a steady purpose—a point on which the
soul may fix its intellectual eye."*

MARY SHELLEY

Ancient Wisdom

Psychologists are beginning to see and accept the meaning of ancient wisdom. Religious leaders have always known about it, but they have not stressed the value and importance as strongly as they might have.

"It is done unto you as *you believe*," is one of the most powerful phrases uttered by the sage of Bethlehem. Nowadays the medical profession is acknowledging that the healing power of the mind is awesome. Placebos work as well as the real thing nearly 50 percent of the time because the people taking the sugar pills believe in their potency. The strength comes from *within* us, not from the outside.

The same concept holds true in business and in personal relationships. If you believe you will be accepted, you usually are. If you believe an interview or a date will go badly, it most often does.

Since belief and faith are often used interchangeably, we should examine our level of conviction when we want something to happen. If our faith is strong, we will generally prevail. If it is weak, we defeat ourselves.

Or, as the wise men of India say: "What goes around, comes around."

GRRRR...

Do you:
GRoan
GRovel
GRipe
GRimace
GRowl?

If these illustrations strike home, look at these words which will negate the above:

GRatitude
GReat
GReet
GRow
GRateful.

Our attitudes should remind us that we are God's GReatest miracle, and as such we don't have to grieve, grimace or growl at the hand life has dealt us.

A GRateful attitude permits us to concentrate on the resolution to those complaints. A *solution-oriented* person will look for ways to relabel a cause and call it a "challenge" or "opportunity" for personal growth instead of a barrier.

We are never handed a problem unless the seeds for its correction are already within us. We just need to water them by using creative thinking and clearing the cobwebs from our minds.

To change your GRowls to purrs, GReet each day with a smile.

Replace GReed with GRatitude. Be GRateful for opportunities that come your way. Turn a GRumpy attitude into a GReat one.

People who know me have long stopped asking, "How are you, Jacques?"

They know the answer will always be "GRRRReat! But I'll get *better!*"

Synergy

Synergy: working together.

Working and living together is not as difficult as one might imagine. In order to know what others think and feel, just look within *yourself*. What you need and want, we *all* need and want. The emotions which drive you also drive others. We all share what is called the "collective unconscious." (Carl Jung)

The following examples best explain synergy:

- A symphony orchestra—100 different instruments playing in harmony.
- A relay team—four swimmers or runners sprinting in turn to win.
- A chorus—a multitude of voices blending into a delightful melody.
- A team of sales reps—a dozen men and women all working to sell the same product and make their company great.
- The cast of a television show—actors putting forth their best to garner good ratings.

"We have learned that we cannot live alone; that our own wellbeing is dependent on the well-being of other nations, far away," said Franklin Delano Roosevelt at his fourth inaugural address in 1945. "We have learned to be citizens of the world, members of the human community."

Nearly half a century later we are still playing out his credo. Don't be too concerned with other nations far away at this time. Just begin where you are. Get involved with others, working in synergistic union to move forward.

Synergy *multiplies* our power, just as the closed fist is more than five times stronger than any of the fingers alone.

Replacing *competition* with *cooperation* leads to greater combined results. Sharing is living, hoarding is existing.

PSI

The week wouldn't be complete without an acronym.

PSI has always been recognized as Per Square Inch. Of course, my PSI stands for Poor Self-Image. On a scale of one to 10, where do you stand? Most people fall at about six.

Do you remember the movie *10* starring Bo Derek and Dudley Moore? She was a definite 10. We don't have to look as gorgeous as Bo, but we are all capable of rising above a six.

Deep within us all are qualities of self-confidence, self-love, selfesteem. Sitting next to those attributes are the negatives of self-hate, guilt, anger, feelings of worthlessness.

Wherever I go I find people who are on a self-destruct mission. These individuals exhibit the worst side of their PSI by making bad business decisions, driving poorly, thus getting into accidents, giving themselves ulcers and other illnesses, causing financial fiascos for themselves and others.

A poor self-image can be turned around once we remember and accept the fact that we are a reflection of our Creator. We need to look inward to study *spiritual economics*—that's where the best interest rates are.

We get out of life what we put in. Likewise, we project to others what we feel about ourselves. Would you rather interact on a business or personal level with someone who has a PSI of three or a PSI of nine? (Nine equals positive self-image.)

If you engage in any type of sports, card games or board games (especially Scrabble), you play up to your opponent's skill and down to their incompetence. So, too, with PSIs. If you surround yourself with friends who have low self-images, you will sink to their level. Conversely, if you hang around with "10s" you, too, will begin to feel better about yourself.

Take a look at the PSI you project and the PSI of those close to you. With a little hard work and mental fortitude you can push that figure up a notch or two.

Good luck.

Diving into Work

Working for others has its up sides and its down sides. A bumper sticker I saw recently said it well: "The worst day of fishing is better than the best day of working."

Be that as it may, most of us work for others for a salary which pays the rent, the car payments, buys groceries and the miscellaneous things that give us pleasure. If one works for others, there are ethics which should be followed.

Loyalty is one. If you take their money, you are accepting responsibility to do the best you can for that company. That means not degrading your employer behind his or her back.

Try to maintain a positive attitude. Accept assignments with good cheer, not scowls. Projecting a negative attitude only compounds the problems and spreads quicker than the plague. You get paid for doing a job, so do it.

Give it your best. Giving 110 percent of your energy will get you further than holding back, even if you don't believe it. It takes some employers longer than others to recognize proficiency. And, unfortunately, some bosses never see it. If you are giving your best and getting nowhere, don't bad-mouth the company. Start looking in the Help Wanted ads.

William E. B. DuBois said: "The return from your work must be the satisfaction which that work brings you… without this… life is hell."

'Nough said.

"Be not afraid of GReatness: some are born GReat, some achieve GReatness and some have GReatness thrust upon them."

WILLIAM SHAKESPEARE

"Growth is the only evidence of life."

JOHN HENRY, CARDINAL NEWMAN

"I studied the lives of great men and famous women, and I found that the men and women who got to the top were those who did the jobs they had in hand, with everything they had of energy and enthusiasm and hard work."

HARRY S. TRUMAN

Spring Back, Fall Ahead

No Rest for the Weary

Since today is Labor Day and I plan to enjoy some much-needed R and R, I am going to throw this vignette in your lap by asking some questions about work—specifically your work.

- Are you happy in your job?
- Do you feel you are working to your full potential?
- Do you contribute without being asked?
- Would you consider yourself a positive asset?
- Are you doing what you always dreamed of doing?
- Are you settling?
- Are you afraid to change jobs?
- Do you stay from inertia or because you like what you do?
- Is the job everything you hoped it would be?
- Are you making enough money?
- Are you supervised or a supervisor?
- How do you like being bossed around?
- Do you boss others with a smile or a snarl?
- Do you feel your qualifications entitle you to more money?
- Are you being held back from promotions by: your boss, the system of advancement, the corporate policy, or *yourself*?
- Do you dream about doing something else?
- Why don't you?

Okay ladies and gents, the ball is in your court. I'm taking the day off while you ponder these profound questions. I'll be back tomorrow to give you some more positive thoughts.

Risk Your Way to Success

"Great deeds are usually wrought at great risk," said the Greek philosopher Herodotus.

To which I add: The greater the risk, the greater the reward.

Of course, venturing with forethought reduces the chance and brings excitement into the equation. A well-planned risk can definitely bring success. Common synonyms include chance, fortune and luck. As an adjective it includes sensitive, delicate and ticklish. As an idiom it means to "go out of one's depth." We can never go out of our true depth since it is limitless and immeasurable.

Going to new depths also means growing to new heights.

Since I am an acronym junkie, I have come up with one for risks:

R is *reason,* the use of the *right* brain for level-headed thinking.
I is intuition, *the* innate intelligence *from the left brain.*
S *synthesizes* both *sides* for optimum application.
K is *knowledge* and when properly used reduces risk to a minimum.
S is the *success* you will experience.

Venturing into unchartered territory is as important in one's personal life as it is in business. To eliminate risk simply study the accepted modes of communication. *Listening* is by far the single greatest technique since it has no inherent risk factors.

Eventually risk-taking becomes risk-making as you develop selfconfidence to calculate what is best for you and pursue it.

As Theodore Roosevelt said: "Far better it is to dare mighty things, to win glorious triumphs, even though checkered by failure… than to live in the gray twilight that knows not victory or defeat."

Judge Not

The Scene: Jacksonville, Florida airport
The Players: A young lady and an elderly man
The Setting: Both are waiting for a delayed flight

The young lady buys a magazine and a box of cookies at one of the airport shops intending to read and nibble while waiting for boarding to begin. She sits down and puts her things on an empty seat between herself and the above-mentioned gentleman. As she starts reading, he reaches into the cookie box and, without asking, takes one. She takes one and he does also. They keep it up until only one remains. He grabs it, breaks it in half, and offers it to the young woman. Instead of taking it, she grabs her possessions and leaves, turning to glare at him.

He is nonplussed and keeps smiling at her.

As she gets ready to board the plane she rummages through her carry-on for her ticket, which she finds under the box of cookies she bought earlier, ergo she was eating *his* cookies.

End of story... except for the lesson: As I understand it, when we judge anyone we are in effect judging ourselves. "Judge not, lest you judge yourself!" would seem an appropriate paraphrase to the old saying.

Judging is a form of criticism and there is too much of it going around. It always swings back to our own inferiority. To the best of my ability I try to accept people as they are. Babies are the finest example of neutrality. They accept everyone on their own merit.

Three Rs

As you may have realized, there are some recurrent themes in this book. I can boil them down into three words: *Repetition reinforces recognition.* The more times a subject appears the more the point is driven home. The baker's dozen of topics that I keep harping on are the most important elements toward motivating yourself—for I can only give the ideas to you, I cannot make you change. The topics:

1. Personal development
2. Self-knowledge
3. Work ethic
4. Love—for self and others
5. Belief system
6. Continued education
7. Goals and purpose
8. Health—mental and physical
9. Family ties
10. Skills
11. Life changes
12. Letting go of the past
13. Planning success

My personal plan of action takes two directions: The first is to stop wasting time reading bad news and trashy books. The second is making my mind a fertile ground for planting new seeds of instruction. To that end I bought numerous cassettes which give me positive affirmations. I play them in my car and as I jog around the block.

The more you do to improve your own self-image, the better you will feel. Go over the checklist outlined above. Make it a plan to pick one a day and work on improving your concept of it.

For instance, if you are reading this book day by day, today will be a Thursday. Try number four—love—and see if you can do three loving things before you go to bed. Think about it—if 100 people were reading this page along with you and each of them did three loving things, what a wonderful world this would be.

Rest in Peace

Aren't you tired of news people digging up old bodies for review? I am. Sometimes I think I'll scream if I hear one more story about Elvis, Marilyn, or JFK. Now they are exhuming the body of past president Zachary Taylor, who died in 1850, to see if he was poisoned. As if it would make a difference.

Why do we have this morbid fascination? Why can't we let them rest in peace?

Reviewing the past is fine *if* it leads to new discoveries or a better future. But regurgitating the past over and over again leads to a sick future—in fact to no future at all for we are too busy living in the past.

Healthy change begins with an understanding of the past, using the experiences as leverage to improve the present and ultimately the future. We should not let it stunt our emotional growth. We must discover the secrets it holds, then let it go.

Learn to live by accepting the fact that certain things were done in the past that you wish could be changed. But they cannot. You must concede this and move on. Once you willingly rid your mind of the negative ideas which have ruled your actions, you can begin the healing process by strengthening your self-worth.

"The past always looks better than what it was," said Finley Peter Dunne. "It's only pleasant because it isn't here."

*"All work and no play makes Jack a dull boy—
and Jill a wealthy widow."*

EVAN ESAR

*"Nothing is really work unless you would rather be
doing something else."*

JAMES M. BARRIE

*"The Good Old Days are neither better nor worse
than the ones we're living through right now."*

ARTIE SHAW

Horoscopes

Every now and then I glance at my horoscope to see what the cosmic forces have in store for me.

Under Gemini I found this one not long ago: "Your eclectic talents lead you in a new career direction."

While I personally don't put much store in these little quips, I did scan the page and noticed something interesting. Under each sun sign were three or four short sentences. The first one of each was on a positive note. Here are a few more:

Detailed plans pay off.

Stage a last-ditch effort and you'll win.

A social obligation turns into a treat.

Game-playing backfires, a straightforward approach is best.

Small risks put you in a position to get tremendous backing.

I couldn't have said these better myself. Basically they are positive affirmations to help get your day started right.

The power of horoscopes, if you believe in them, is that they can put you in a frame of mind to make things happen instead of waiting for life to push you around like a leaf blowing in the wind.

Take charge of your life. Use your daily horoscope as a springboard to success, but only if it is based on optimism.

Kinesics

Kinesics is the study of body movement, or body language. Chances are if you're a sales rep you have already heard of the term and are familiar with its importance. Even if you are not in sales, it is a valuable concept to know.

For example: at the store the sales clerk says "Have a nice day" while turning away from you. The words are correct but the body language betrays the real attitude—toward you and/or the job.

Body language is especially important between parents and children, employers and workers, lovers, spouses, friends. According to research at the University of California at Los Angeles (UCLA), body language accounts for 55 percent of all communication. Words account for only seven!

When someone says "I love you" does he or she look you in the eye, or down at the floor, or are the eyes glued to the television, or a book, or a newspaper? See what I mean?

Nonverbal signals scream out silently. If you can hear the message you are a step ahead of the game.

Words are the thinking tools, body language expresses feelings with or without your knowledge or control.

"No mortal can keep a secret," said Dr. Sigmund Freud, the father of modern psychoanalysis. "If his lips are silent, he chatters with his fingertips; betrayal oozes out of him at every pore."

Problem Solvers

Not long ago I worked with a group of sales reps at a local Metropolitan Life Insurance office. It was billed as a "training session" but I did not train anyone. I offered options, allowing their own innate intelligence to guide them into making new and favorable decisions career-wise.

How often does an employer say he will "train" you for a new job? To train means to bend, prune, tie up, instruct, discipline and drill—all negative ideas.

Instead of "steering" the mind, employers believe in forcing their ideas on others.

A young woman I know, who prides herself on being a problem solver, worked for several years as a bookkeeper at a small bookstore. The boss showed her what to do, then turned all the account books over to her. This young woman devised a quicker, more efficient way to do the billing, accounts receivable and accounts payable. She proceeded to get the job done in half the time.

Years later the boss, who had by then retired, said to this young woman, "You drove me crazy with your headstrong ways." When the woman argued that her method was more efficient, the boss agreed and added, "That's the only reason I didn't fire you!"

There are always new and better ways of approaching a task. Employers should make a mental note today to keep a keen eye open for the innovators in their departments. Those forward-thinking individuals can make everyone look good. IBMoffers cash rewards for ideas that save the company money. They know that great thoughts can blossom if the training is kept to a minimum and the creative intellect allowed to flow.

Keeping an open mind is one of the keys to successful management. Instead of being so busy teaching others "how to," perhaps it would pay off if you let them "want to." Motivation must come from within. A good trainer knows how to draw forth this great human problem-solving quality and nurture it.

P.S. That goes for parents, too! Our first "trainers."

A Tale of Two Monks

Two monks, sworn to chastity, came to a stream where they spotted a beautiful lady who was afraid to cross because of the strong current. One monk picked her up and without a word carried her to the other side. Since the monks had taken a vow of silence that could only be broken at nightfall, the second monk could not vent his anger.

As the sun set, the second turned to the first and demanded an explanation for his friend's action.

"What? Are you still carrying that woman in your mind?" answered the first monk innocently. "I let her go early this morning."

Are you still carrying the past in your mind and heart? I make it a practice to take a daily scan through my thoughts for remnants of the past that I can let go of—dirty laundry or worn-out records that I no longer need.

Ten years ago I learned a great lesson. After giving a lecture on prosperity at a Science of Mind Center, I began to study their literature. What struck me most was that I discovered the power to forgive lay in my hands. When I began to forgive myself for my past errors, and there were many, I found a new freedom I never experienced before. I began to feel validated as a human being.

As a result I reclaimed my life. I wrenched it from the past and filled it with power, passion and purpose. Instead of looking to the past or the future, I began living in the present.

Let me ask you again—do you dwell in the past? Are you consumed with anger over things you cannot possibly change—whether they were done by you or to you?

If so, take time today to pull up one incident and only one. Study it as the day progresses and vow to let it go, to put it outside the trapdoor to your mind and into the trash. Just that small step will help you down the road to mental freedom and spiritual health.

The Ego and the Cosmos

Pulitzer prize-winning astronomer, Carl Sagan, has written a dozen books and hundreds of scientific papers about the heavens. Whenever my ego begins to swell, I pick up a book called *Cosmos* and start reading.

Did you know there are 100 billion galaxies, each containing an average of 100 billion stars? How can my little mass of gray matter compare to that?

We are unraveling the secrets of the universe at breakneck speed. It makes me feel quite humble—and yet, it is only a three-pound tool (that mass of gray matter) that is being used.

I would not trade my brain for all the computers in the world. For they cannot think, feel or create. They can only do what we humans tell them to do.

As Albert Einstein said: "The whole of science is nothing more than a refinement of everyday thinking."

This means that you and I have both the scientist and artist lurking in the recesses of our mind. I try to let mine expand whenever possible, but I also try not to let it get out of control. I certainly don't want to be pegged as a "know-it-all." Even Carl Sagan, who has one of the most brilliant minds of this century, does not posture like a peacock. He is quite an affable fellow, presenting his highly scientific discoveries not in highbrow language, but in a way we can all understand. That is to his credit. He doesn't have to laud his intelligence over us.

Do you? If you have to be right, to be the smartest, the most clever, the best, think about Carl Sagan and the 100 billion galaxies out there. Certainly that should put things in perspective for you. There are many ways to be right, to be the smartest, to be the best.

We are all just a tiny, tiny part of a vast cosmos. Let us try not to forget that simple fact.

"You don't get a second chance at a first impression."

WILL ROGERS

"Remember happiness doesn't depend upon who you are or what you have; it depends solely upon what you think."

DALE CARNEGIE

"The no-mind not-thinks no-thoughts about no-things."

BUDDHA

The Dead Zone

The "dead zone" or "comfort zone" is known in the heating and air conditioning trades as 72 degrees. It is the area where neither cooling nor heating takes place.

Most humans live in a dead zone since they only use 2 percent of their natural abilities. They meander—wandering aimlessly or casually with no urgent destination—letting life take them where it may.

Living in the dead zone is like being a goldfish in a six-inch bowl—swimming in circles getting nowhere. Most of us will rationalize our lives and defend our right to stay like that forever.

This kind of thinking reminds me of the great Albert Einstein when he said: "Only two things are infinite: the universe and human stupidity—and I'm not sure about the former."

Some of the ideas which keep us in this dead/comfort zone include:

Guilt

Fear

Hate

Feelings of unworthiness

The past

We tend to forget that every day is a new day and we need not drag our old garbage into it. Most of us are proud of our old neuroses which inhibit personal growth and achievement. We display the reasons we should stay average or mediocre and expect others to support our delusions.

Every time I lecture, a number of people confront me during the break and say they do not have problems with low self-image. I agree. They don't have a dilemma because they choose to acknowledge it. They accept it as part of their being—which is true. They have made it a reality.

I once heard someone say: Those who can do, and those who *won't* criticize.

I wrote won't instead of can't because we all can. If we truly want to change we can all get out of our dead zone and into the arena of life.

Begin at the Beginning

On my way back from a seminar I noticed a new bumper sticker. It read: "If you can't see my mirror I can't see you."

It reminded me that most of us cannot "see" God residing within ourselves. We are blind to his manifestation.

At my next seminar I tried an experiment. I handed out mirrors and asked the people in the group to look into them and affirm their selflove and self-acceptance exactly as they were at that moment. Most had difficulty—some could not even look into their own eyes (what are they hiding?). Likewise they have trouble greeting each day.

Every morning they drag their bodies out of bed, struggle through a sugar-laced breakfast, and straggle through the day with their minds on automatic pilot. They exchange complaints with co-workers, work unhappily at their jobs, then return home for a dinner which they cannot taste, and slide onto the couch where they remain until they drag themselves into bed, taking their worries along with them.

If I just described your daily routine, it's time for a radical change. Start at the beginning.

First, think about your reason for being here on Earth. Is it to act like a sponge, soaking up the energy around you without making any type of meaningful contribution? Or are you a prisoner in your mental jail waiting for someone to turn the key and release you? If you are, you'll wait forever. Nobody can liberate you except *you*.

Don't wear your mind like an old pair of slippers, shuffling through life just because it feels comfortable.

Start each day with a purpose, a goal, something to work toward as the hours creep by. I believe that you will find each day has an added dimension you never thought possible.

I don't expect that by the end of the month you will have effected a complete makeover, just take it from the beginning, waking up with an improved attitude, taking those feelings to work, back home, and using them during the evening to improve the quality of your life.

Remember my wise words: The time to grow is now, the place to grow is here, the person to grow is you!

Born a Winner, Died a Whiner

That epitaph should be on one out of five tombstones. It is approximately the ratio of people who *make* things happen versus *allowing* them to happen.

The losers go around "iff-ing" their way through life, blaming their lack of personal fulfillment on others and on circumstances saying "if, if, if." They continue to lead with their chin instead of learning from their experiences to duck when they see trouble coming.

On his maiden trip from England to New York, Emmett Fox, the eminent theologian and philosopher, went into a cafeteria and sat down. He waited and waited for someone to take his order, not realizing it was *self-serve* style. Finally, succumbing to his hunger, he looked around and watched people line up and take their own food. He followed suit. He never forgot this lesson and often preached about it from the pulpit. This is a self-service world.

There are few limits imposed on us by nature. The majority of us are free from disabilities. We can become whatever we want. But we must dip into the bag of gifts handed to us by our Creator. Gifts don't jump out at us (unless we are lucky enough to win the lottery—even then we must first buy a ticket).

Whining and wallowing in self-pity is destructive like a car running in reverse—or not running at all.

As Auntie Mame said: "Life is a banquet and some poor sons-of bitches are starving to death."

The winners and the whiners are both in the cafeteria of life. They can choose to starve or they can feast on the delicacies provided.

To quote Ben Franklin: "Some people die at 25 and aren't buried until they are 75!"

Hey, let's not get too comfortable.

Three Giants

This vignette concerns three giants in the field of humanities—separated in time by almost 25 centuries.

The first is Socrates, the ancient Greek philosopher, who promoted the theory that only virtuous actions produce lasting happiness (or that a person's self-interest is best served by always doing the right thing).

The second is Dr. Hans Selye of the University of Montreal, a world authority on stress. His theory is called "altruistic egoism" and involves the theory that we can earn true freedom and peace of mind through unselfish acts performed for others.

Third is Mihaly Csikszentmihalyi, a modern-day philosopher whose current bestseller, *Flow, the Psychology of Optimal Experience*, promotes his theory on "autotelic self." Literally it means a person has self-contained goals—they come from within and are based on intuition, inspiration and insight. These qualities are inherited at birth and, when used in the outside world, lead to winners (not whiners).

All three philosophies are designed to help us lead happy, stress-free lives. If we take these experts at face value, it means we were born to love, to give and to grow to full maturity. The more we create in our lives, the more will come back to refill us.

Tasks

As the week draws to a close, I'd like to give you a few exercises in self-improvement:

1. Write this phrase down on two pieces of paper: "Whatever my mind can conceive and believe, I can achieve." Okay, now put one paper on the refrigerator and one in your wallet. Every day next week take a second in the morning and a few seconds every time you open your wallet to re-read the message. Come to believe the words you have written.
2. Praise yourself for something you've done (or haven't done, if it's negative) every morning and every night. If you've done something terrific really praise yourself. Each day is made of hundreds of large and small decisions and actions. Be proud of the ones that turned out well.
3. Before you go to bed at night, make a list of the things you wanted to do but didn't. Then write next to them the reason why they were not done. Was it time? Did you shuffle important things to the back burner? Or did you deliberately hold yourself in check, making some excuse? Then make a "to do" list and plan to tackle the most difficult tasks the following day. Start with the hard ones so you can put them behind you. Save the most pleasant chores for the end. That way you won't go through the day with a negative attitude.
4. Let go of the things that did not go well. You can do nothing about the past. Program that negative thinking out of the cerebral computer immediately. Don't let it become part of your psyche.

With those tasks in place, enjoy the weekend.
Stay positive, stay focused.
See you on Monday.

"Life is just one damned thing after another."
　　　　　　　　　　　FRANK WARD O'MALLEY

"The future enters into us, in order to transform itself in us, long before it happens."
　　　　　　　　　　　RAINER MARIA RILKE

Where Are You?

This morning in the Ziggy cartoon, he was looking at a sign that read "You Are Here." He had a puzzled look on his face.

Do you know where you are? I don't mean physically—what street, town or state. I mean do you know where you are in life? Are you coming or going? Are you up or down? Are you inside or outside?

We are all traveling down the road of experience. Some of us have a clear idea where we are headed. Others are caught in a fog. Some of us have our lights on illuminating the way. Others have blinders on, keeping them from seeing the opportunities that can lead off the well-worn path into new adventures. Some of us travel like the tortoise, plodding slowly and surely along the route to our eventual demise. Others are like the jackrabbit, leaping from venture to venture, never settling down on one thing and making a success of it.

To all of the above situations, there must be a happy medium. It is fine to know where we are headed. But we cannot shut out chance encounters that may guide us to new and exciting adventures. While it is commendable to be faithful to a company for 30 years, I always wonder about those who retire never having tried something new or different. I don't suggest the jackrabbit routine, for nothing really gets accomplished with that type of attitude. Perhaps a little jumping around at first, then settling down into a routine that will move you along to career success, always staying alert to new opportunities.

So where are you on this fine September morning? Are you bouncing around from job to job, never applying yourself and your energy to one passion? Or are you the plowhorse with blinders on?

Where are you and where are you going?

I'm Okay, You're Okay

We are bombarded daily by advertisements—on the radio and television, in newspapers and magazines. They are intended to make us buy things. But what they really do is make us feel self-conscious, unattractive, unhealthy, and dissatisfied with our beings and our possessions.

Think about the ads that say you have bad breath, body odor, discolored teeth, rattling dentures. The ads with svelte young women and muscular-bodied men make us feel too fat, too skinny, too old, with too little hair on our heads and too much on our bodies.

Our homes are not exempt from this barrage: The carpets are musty, the baby's room smells, we have germs everywhere and dust mites. Our cars, of course, are never fast or powerful enough, they don't have pickup or cornering ability, they cannot climb buildings or mountains, or haul 20 tons of bricks.

And now I ask you, if you could eliminate all those ads that make you feel inadequate, would you like yourself exactly the way you are?

Instead of being reminded constantly of our shortcomings, wouldn't it be wonderful if we were praised for all the good things we represent—if that spark of divinity that's in each of us was recognized. If nobody else will tell you, I will.

You are great. You are terrific. You are uniquely special. There is always room for improvement. It is up to you to decide where you need it. Nobody has the right to make you feel bad about yourself. Not the advertisers, not your spouse, not your boss or your children.

Remember the book *I'm O.K., You're O.K.?* That pretty much sums it up.

Educare

Educare comes from Latin and means to draw forth from within. I would like to change the spelling to edu-CARE, meaning whether we draw forth innate abilities or teach structured information, we put more CARE into the effort.

The less we instruct (a left brain function) and the more we draw from intuitive knowledge (a right brain function), the better the student will learn to handle life's challenges. Studies have shown that concentrating on people skills, instead of career skills, when a child is in the formative years will lead to success in life, whatever profession a person chooses.

While most teachers are devoted to their occupation and care for the students, there is a certain amount of apathy and cynicism that creeps in year after year. The kids these days are harder to teach, filled with anger and "attitude;" the classes are larger, the time shorter. Most instructors try their best, but today one's best isn't always good enough. And it is difficult leaving one's own personal problems at home, not letting them interfere with the teaching process.

It wouldn't hurt to have refresher courses once or twice a year to assist teachers in dealing with the unhappy campers in their classes—just like the seminars I facilitate for customer service representatives.

We must learn to care about others, to put our own personal difficulties aside and reach inside young minds and hearts, and thus draw forth their full potential.

NLP Revisited

I first read about Neuro-Linguistic Programming (NLP) fourteen years ago. NLP basically places full responsibility for clear communication on the sender, not the receiver. I think this makes sense.

Do you make sense when you speak? Are your messages clear or confused, concise or contradictory?

If you've ever traveled in a foreign country and tried to speak their language, you know how difficult it can be to get an idea across. And although two people speak the same language, the message doesn't always cross the linguistic gap correctly. That's when misinterpretations occur.

Think about the number of times you have given directions and not had them followed correctly, or conversely, been given directions and been chastised because you did not follow them properly.

I have found that whenever directions are being given to me, it is best to repeat them back to the sender.

"Jacques, mow the closet then clean the lawn," says Carole.

"Yes, dear. You want me to mow the closet then clean the lawn?"

"Oh, did I say that? No, I meant clean the closet and mow the lawn."

See how simple it is. I saved myself a ton of work. Imagine what my wife would have said if I had followed her direction and mowed the closet. She would have thought I'd lost my mind. But I would have been following her directions to the letter. By repeating back her instructions, I saved hours of labor and probably a huge argument, too.

It is so easy to derail the train of thoughts. Words are the switches which keep us going in the proper direction. They avoid collisions with the thoughts and ideas of others.

Sounds of Love

They begin in the bedroom, and they involve my two favorite ladies. Both are white, middle-aged, and petite. It is 6:32 A.M., and the only noise coming from the bedroom are the sounds of my wife, Carole, and our dog, Sam (Samantha), gently snoring. One is lying on the bed, the other under the bed. I trust you don't have to guess who is lying where. Once in a while I hear another kind of sound coming from under the bed. It reaches me in the form of little "yips" and continues on for several minutes. It's Samantha having one of her dreams with unpleasant overtones... a nightmare no doubt. Meanwhile, my wife continues to snore while safely nestled in my arms.

Samantha is a Shih Tzu. She is the quietest dog who ever owned me. Who else but an owner could weigh a scant 12 pounds yet control my life to such a large degree? Who else could force me out of my warm, cozy home during a snow storm just so she could go for a "walk" to her favorite toilet? Who else makes me dress up in several layers of cotton, wool and polyester just to keep from freezing any part of my anatomy? Samantha wears her fur coat indoors as well as outside no matter what the weather.

Since Sam is a non-barker, saving it for what she considers real emergencies only, we do not always know when she needs to take her walk so we've learned to watch her body language. We're pretty sure she wants to go out when she sits by the front door and looks at one of us expectantly. Or, she goes into the kitchen and sits by her leash, which she uses to control me when we're outside. After all, who knows what sort of trouble I might get I to when left to my own devices.

Getting back once again to the sounds of love, I find it very reassuring when I hear one or both of them gently snoring. When Sam occasionally lets go with a deep sigh I know she just fulfilled or gave up on a special wish she harbored during the day. My special wish is to continue to hear the sounds of love from both my ladies for many years to come. Sigh!

Question! What love sounds do *you* resonate to?

"I can resist everything except temptation."
OSCAR WILDE

"Wit and wisdom are born with a man."
JOHN SELDON

TUNA

A man sat next to a co-worker in the lunchroom one day and unwrapped a tuna fish sandwich. He turned to his friend and said: "I hate tuna!"

"Why don't you ask your wife to fix you something else?" asked the friend.

"I can't," answered the sandwich eater. "I've been fixing my own lunch for the past 20 years."

Question: Have you been fixing your lunch (i.e., your life) the same way for all these years, then complaining about the taste?

Let me tell you right now that *you* plan the menu. You might not be able to change the restaurant, but you can make something different for breakfast, lunch and dinner every day of your life—and I'm not talking about food.

Look around at your co-workers, see how creative they can be. If you notice something you like, try it yourself. Create new recipes from the ingredients that make up our everyday existence. Add gusto, add spice, put some relish in the tuna.

TUNA in my lexicon stands for Totally Unacceptable Negative Attitude. Negatives belong in a darkroom, not in your day-to-day activities. Bad attitudes and feelings are passed down from generation to generation for centuries until someone puts the brakes on. That person can be you. Making the right choices is like picking from the menu at a Chinese restaurant—a little of this from column A, and a little of that from column B. Then, once the decision is made, enjoy the flavors.

The challenge for this week is to try something new every day—and no tuna, please.

Storm Warnings

Stretch Marks

During my 20 years of lecturing I have worked with many sales organizations and service clubs. Part of my routine has been to ask for a volunteer to come to the front of the class and reach up as high as he or she can. Once in the stretch position, I ask the volunteer to stretch even *higher*. I usually get an additional two to four inches.

When the volunteer is safely tucked back in his or her seat I ask what it was all about. Mostly I get puzzled looks and shrugs. Then I explain that the first reach indicates their self-image and the final reach—that extra few inches—is the person's *untapped potential.*

I usually suggest they make the higher reach their new goal by developing it into a habit. In practice this means increased training in all areas, but more importantly it means changing one's attitude toward oneself based on self-admiration and self-love.

Improving skills such as speaking, listening and using a telephone properly will help increase sales as well as improve interpersonal relations at work and at home.

So make it a practice to reach *higher,* stretch your abilities those extra inches. It will make you a bigger and better person.

Brainwashing

Today, if you are an average person, you will use up 57,600 seconds being awake. During that time you will be bombarded by more than 18,000 messages—one every 3.2 seconds. If you go to the supermarket, you will be besieged by more than 24,000 products. And this is only the beginning. Futurists say that it will get worse.

And yet there is hope. As the great Frenchman Alphonse Karr said: "The more things change, the more they remain the same."

The more the outer trappings of the world shift, the more effort it will take for us to remain constant and in control. Too many of us feel frightened and helpless because of the problems brought about by the ills of society. We are easily distressed, the pressure is on, we are cynical and anxious.

We need good news on a daily basis in order to stay afloat emotionally. During the 57,600 seconds you are awake each day, make it your business to find some positive energy—from a walk, a sporting event, an upbeat nonviolent movie (are there any?), music, my tapes (!), a self-help book, a lively discussion with a friend, a craft course, etc.

There are loads of pleasant things to see and do during your waking hours. Take advantage of them, add up the positives, delete the negatives.

A Kinder, Gentler Time

My wife and I were driving from New York to the Poconos in the hills of Pennsylvania. The differences soon became apparent.

In New York we were told to pay for gas *before* filling up. In the Poconos we were told to pay for gas *after* filling up.

In New York the bathrooms were locked. In the Poconos they are left unlocked.

In New York, you pay and go as though you don't exist. In the Poconos the clerk and owner both *thanked* me! That's when I realized a kinder gentler world does exist right here in America.

I think that we become so conditioned to rude and erratic behavior that we are desensitized. We are hardened to others less fortunate—the disabled, the elderly, homeless people and even criminals. A kind word or action can go a long way in making this world a better place for all of us to live.

Remember when I wrote about synergy—working together. We need the combined energy of all the millions of Americans to make America the type of country it once was—where people helped their neighbor instead of suing them.

I believe we must embrace the philosophy that all of us are created equal in God's eyes. I believe we need to erase state boundaries and learn to think of America as one huge colorful quilt.

Polyticks

No, this is not a misspelling. It's a metaphor I chose to illustrate today's politics.

Polyticks, or many ticks, remind me of politicians as a genre. Both a tick and a politician latch onto their victim, then drain them dry.

A famous wit once remarked that if we took all politicians and lined them up on the ground, touching head to toe for miles on end, it would be a wonderful thing. Period.

Voting, in this humble writer's opinion, has become a question of choosing the lesser of two evils. I have become disillusioned with the phrase "the will of the people." The American public has become like the guy wearing a billboard on his back that says "kick me."

There are honest men and women serving the government. Unfortunately, I believe they are in the minority. I just want to be able to vote and sleep nights knowing the job is being done according to the promises made.

I'm not the only cynic when it comes to this topic.

Frank McKinney Hubbard said: "Now and then an innocent man is sent to the legislature."

Louis McHenry Howe added: "You cannot adopt politics as a profession and remain honest."

And the great satirist Will Rogers sums it up: "This country has come to feel the same when Congress is in session as when the baby gets hold of a hammer."

"If there is but little water in the stream, it is the fault not of the channel, but of the source."

SAINT JEROME

"The short memories of American voters is what keeps our politicians in office."

WILL ROGERS

School

According to a recent survey of 100 students at the University of Miami, nearly 50 percent did not know where London was. Of the same 100, eight could not find Miami—although they were in Miami at the time! Many Americans think New Mexico is part of the country Mexico and not one of the 50 states in the Union.

While more young adults are attending college than ever, they are dropping out by the droves—nearly half who start will never finish.

Even more alarming, three out of four high school students admit to cheating. In college that figure rises to one out of two!

The attitudes of teachers and pupils run parallel—they have low expectations of achievement and low motivation. One problem is that we concentrate more on "Fs" like facts, figures and formulas and not enough on "As" like appreciation, acceptance and approval.

Mediocrity is becoming the norm these days. Teachers are encouraged to pass children to the next level although they are not equipped to handle the more advanced work. Remedial classes are increased to take care of the overload. Class activities include games and low-level instruction just to keep the kids occupied until they can graduate. But what are they to do once they complete their education? How can they compete? The answer is they can't.

The responsibility falls on both parents and educators to make sure children get positive feedback. Learning should be pleasurable and fun. Enthusiasm must be present in the classroom to keep tedium away.

Young minds are like parachutes. We only get one chance to open them the right way.

If parents and teachers work together their energy resembles a tandem bike, with all effort going in the same direction at the same time. The result is optimum. Conversely, when a teacher pats the back of a child and the parent beats it, the child is confused and demoralized. The same goes for teachers who berate their pupils in an effort to make them learn by humiliation. That is not acceptable instruction.

The apple may not fall far from the tree, but if it lies on the ground and is not properly nourished it will rot.

48 Hours

When is a three-day weekend not a three-day weekend? The answer to this riddle is, when it's only 48 hours long.

We began our three-day weekend on a Friday at one in the afternoon. We returned on Sunday at one in the afternoon. The time in between was spent at a rustic inn in the Poconos, enjoying simple homemade cuisine and wallowing in the beauty of the environment as the leaves turned from green to golden brown. It was truly awesome.

Since we spent part of Friday, all of Saturday and part of Sunday at the Overlook Inn, it was called a three-day weekend. But in reality our stay was only 48 hours.

To this revelation I say, so be it. I try to make all trips, whether for business or pleasure, as pleasant as possible. It's an *attitude* thing. Positive thinking propels me forward into a cheerful time instead of a nightmare.

So when you travel, and, yes even the commute to work counts, put your outlook into forward gear and enjoy yourself—even if it's only Tuesday.

Our Ps and Rs

Fifty years ago I came here as a war refugee. At the time, America was the role model for the world with Pride, Purpose and Patriotism spreading throughout the globe, inspiring others.

Only half a century later, the three Ps have become Perks, Prescriptions and Procrastination.

We are now world leaders in crime, suicide, abortions, teen pregnancies, substance abuse problems, divorce and prison overcrowding. Pretty gruesome statistics, don't you think? We have lost our economic and educational edges.

These days Reading, wRiting and 'Rithmetic have become Ritual, Rut and Routine. Our national motto could well become "What's in it for me?"

I cried in 1943 when I first saw the Statue of Liberty. Those were tears of joy. Now I cry because my dream of America the magnificent has been shattered. I have come to the sad conclusion that morality these days has a high degree of mortality.

Rudeness has replaced respect.

Raises are more important than an honest day's work.

Rules ride roughshod over initiative.

Racial discrimination is on the rise.

As rotten as it sounds, there is a way to turn things around.

What we need to do is to Raise our self-esteem, put Religion back into our lives and show Respect to others.

People Classifier

Not long ago I received a brochure from the National Institute of Business Management which is called a Customer Classifier and Analyzer. I have changed it to a People Classifier, since we are all customers of sorts.

The object of this selling tool is to offer the salesperson an instant appraisal of the potential customer. It conveniently classifies consumers into 18 neat pigeonholes so the salesperson knows the proper approach to take.

They include:

- The Skeptic
- The Gabber
- The Clam
- The Chameleon
- The Bargainer
- The Arguer
- The Pessimist

When my wife and son and I tried to pigeonhole ourselves, we failed miserably. We all have *combinations* of these traits.

A rotating wheel within this device offers the best way to handle the customer. Each type has 10 different approaches you can take. Since the salesperson can't take the tool when he or she goes on a call, all 18 types, each with 10 possibilities for a sales pitch, must be memorized.

It also means you must be able to instantly "peg" the person so you can proceed without hesitation.

Question: If this system is so effective, why are sales reps still only closing one sale out of five presentations?

The answer is manipulation instead of integrity. Pegging your pigeon and going for the kill will usually backfire if there is no product belief and consideration for the people involved.

Honesty and hard work always sell better than trickery. Yes, I know it's an old-fashioned idea. But people are people and must be taken on their own merits or demerits. No new-fangled Customer Classifier gizmo can do that for you.

Dinosaurs

The stegosaurus was a prehistoric creature with a tiny brain and a huge tail with spikes that it used to bash the brains out of its prey. Some of us are just like that dinosaur—we act before we think. As a result we confuse activity with accomplishment—there's a lot of action but very little progress.

According to *Reader's Digest*, our interests in order of importance are:

- Health
- Wealth
- Self-improvement
- Marriage
- Desire for advancement.

Seems we are guilty of some backward thinking. There is nothing wrong with wanting health and wealth, marriage and advancement. The problem is that we put self-improvement in the middle instead of at the beginning. This is the *only one* that can help us attain the others. It should be the cornerstone of our lives.

Self-improvement is deeply rooted in the ethics taught by the great philosophers throughout the ages—Plato, Aristotle, Kant, Mill and others.

For this weekend, make a list of your interests in order of importance. Then take a critical look at how you have placed them. Where does self-improvement fall in your list?

"Example is the school of mankind, and they will learn at no other."

EDMUND BURKE

"If the blind lead the blind, both shall fall into the ditch."

MATTHEW 15:14

"By perseverance the snails reached the ark."

CHARLES HADDON

Bumped

It took the resignation of a Supreme Court justice to knock me off the "Good Morning America" show.

In June 1986, Warren E. Berger stepped down from a post which he had held for 17 years. His news was more important than mine, so I got bumped to the Regis Philbin show instead.

What caused me to become the national celebrity of the moment? I was the first male in the history of New York State to become president of a women's business club.

I felt it was a victory over sexual discrimination. Unfortunately *Newsday* magazine did not see it that way and, after interviewing me, decided not to run the story. Bumped again!

However, I was featured on the evening news for both ABC and CBS—only after they had exhausted their slew of bad news. I counted 11 items on one station and 10 on the other. Then came my chance to turn things around to a positive note. But I'm sure if there had been another gruesome item, I would have been bumped once more.

The bad news in the papers outdistances the good news 9.5 to one. As a nation, we are heading into an abyss of pessimism which could eventually consume us all.

I believe we are all created in God's spiritual image and we should act in a honorable and dignified manner at all times.

I'm sorry I was bumped from the "Good Morning America" show. It would have been a wonderful opportunity to impart some positive feelings to millions of Americans.

Body Betrayal

After reading a new book on human communication, I wonder how I manage to get my ideas across to others, whether one-on-one or in front of a thousand eager attendees. The book was written by two Ph.D.'s and should best be read by other Ph.D.'s who will be able to make sense of it.

There were some interesting facts, however, that even a layperson like me can understand.

Did you know that according to the study of kinesics (body language) there are 700,000 ways to transmit signs using only the body? For example, your eyebrows alone can send out 23 separate signals depending on their positioning at the time someone is looking at you. This little fact certainly raised *my* eyebrows!

Nonverbal researchers also investigated these oddly named areas of communication:

- Oculesics—the study of eye behavior.
- Haptics—the role of touch.
- Vocalis—the use of voice (also known as para-language).
- Cronemics—how we handle objects.

Having my own Ph.D. (a Philosopher's Dedication), I find that the proper use of intuitive skills will invariably out-perform the mastery of these 700,000 versions of bodily communication.

The tried and true methods of human interaction will usually get the job done. Once we understand the dynamics of personal motivation and its various components, our messages will have clear sailing.

By the timely use of empathy, sympathy, praise, love and recognition, along with the use of the obvious body language signs, we will be able to solve problems quickly and efficiently. We will raise communication to new and unbelievable heights.

Spiritual Poverty

America, the land of religious freedom, is slowly dying of spiritual poverty. As a nation, we are entering moral bankruptcy.

I believe there are as many real reasons for our national decline as there are opinions about its causes. These include the new morality used by businesses and education, where cheating is permitted as long as you don't get caught.

Crime is growing faster than the population. Old values are not being taught to new generations. We seem to have an obsession with the past, but only the bad part.

I know people who still harbor deep hatred for the Japanese for bombing Pearl Harbor. Others still refuse to buy any German-made or Japanese-made products.

Anger, revenge and loathing clog the lines of creativity. The burners are *on*, but the pilot light is *off* and nothing is cooking.

Loving yourself and others cannot start until the anger is dissolved.

I can only hope that this nation will pull itself out of its spiritual vacuum and get back on track so we can start raising a new generation of caring, sharing and morally upright young men and women.

Networking for Success

Networking (working the nets) was a 16th century method of catching fish. Today networking is used to capture new prospects, information or resources. More succinctly put:

She who has a thing to sell
And goes and whispers in a well
Is not so apt to get the dollars
As she who climbs a tree and hollers.

The more people who know who you are and what you do, the easier it will be for you to reach new heights in selling.

I haven't had an acronym for a while so here's one for you:

N is for *nurturing* your client base.

E is for becoming an *expert* and *exchanging* cards with others.

T is for *training* and, of course, the *telephone.*

W *is for* who, what, when, where *and* why. Work *your leads.*

O is for *offering* to speak at *organizations* and keeping in touch with *old* clients.

R is for *role* models. Become one.

K is for *knowledge* which leads to power sales. *Know* your business.

I *is for* interacting, initiating *and* interest *in others.*

N is for *need,* help fill those of your clients.

G is for *goals.* And don't forget *God* who watches over all of us.

In the business world, networking comes before selling. In a recent survey of the selling process here are the predictable results:

The approach was the most difficult for 3 percent of those polled. The presentation was hardest for 6 percent. The closing was toughest for 10 percent. But nearly 50 percent admitted that networking was the hardest to master. Many people in business don't like being rejected so they don't put themselves on the line.

You can overcome the Networking Blues by knowing that you are just as capable and likeable as the next person, maybe more so. A few rejections won't hurt. Keep your eye on the prize and a lilt in your voice, and you'll soon network right into success.

Self-Criticism

In a motivational counseling session with two co-workers I used this technique. I asked them to make two lists for me. The first was an appraisal of their personal liabilities and assets. The second list was to describe the liabilities and assets of their fellow worker. Here are the results:

CLIENT A (about himself):	CLIENT B (about A):
I am a procrastinator	You are caring, concerned
I don't like criticism	You are emotional, funny
I hate to follow up	You are intelligent
I yell too much	You are loving and happy

CLIENT B (about himself):	CLIENT A (about B):
I am too fat	You are sweet, loving
I am not efficient	You are caring, honest
I am shy and opinionated	You are trustworthy
I am lazy	You are happy, sincere

Do we enjoy this self-flagellation? Why would we find so many negatives and so few positives about ourselves? Why do we appreciate the good qualities in others but ignore those same qualities within us?

When asked, the clients said that self-praise is not proper. I say it is essential to good mental health. Your self-esteem will grow geometrically as you applaud yourself. Take a bow! Now!

Remember, there are no perfect people. We are all trying to discard our imperfections. The most effective way to do this is to spend your time thinking optimistically. This will help create favorable conditions as the subconscious veers away from the negative and toward the positive.

This weekend, make your own list. Don't spare the positive attributes.

And remember Dr. Norman Vincent Peale's classic saying: "The only people that I have ever known to have no problems are in the cemetery."

"We are all here for a spell; get all the good laughs you can."

WILL ROGERS

"Prejudice not founded on reason cannot be removed by argument."

SAMUEL JOHNSON

"By the street of By-and-By, one arrives at the House-of-Never."

MIGUEL DE CERVANTES

Taking Inventory

Before I packed for my aforementioned vacation in the Poconos, I put together a mental list of the things I would need. Then I began packing.

Starting from my feet and working upward, I took out socks, shoes, trousers, underwear, shirts, belt, jacket. Then I headed into the bathroom for my personal articles—shaving cream, razor and blades, comb, etc.

I spend many days a year traveling so this has become fairly routine. Nevertheless, when I am finished and ready to close the suitcase, I always step back and take an inventory, just to make sure I've got everything.

When was the last time you took an inventory—not of the clothes in your closet, but of *yourself*? When did you last make a list of your assets—strengths, talents and abilities? If you've been following this book the way it was meant to be read, you did that on Friday. How did you do?

Writing down how you think and feel about yourself is therapeutic. It allows you to study the final product and use it as a jumping off point for making serious personality adjustments.

Read over the good points you jotted down and memorize them. Make them part of your everyday routine, reinforce that self-respect, let it boost your self-confidence.

Use the negative list to begin making changes. As you work through each unsatisfactory trait, cross it off. Hopefully, with diligence, you will wind up with an inventory of positive attributes.

Once you love yourself, you can truly begin to love others.

Being

"To be or not to be," is one of William Shakespeare's most famous sayings. But what does it mean? Linguistic experts and philosophers have been debating this for centuries. Here is my interpretation.

To become means to change, something that happens in the future. To become indicates an attempt. The problem with this concept is that while one hopes it will succeed, there is always the possibility it will fail.

On the other hand, to be means to live in the *present*. That means one *is*.

A major difference between become and be lies in our personal attitudes toward life. Those who wait to become are, in effect, procrastinators while those who choose to be are acting in the moment—taking possession of the now and using it to advantage.

Many great thinkers have made note of the past, the present and the future.

- Ralph Waldo Emerson: "What lies behind us and what lies before us are tiny matters compared to what is in us."
- Samuel Taylor Coleridge: "And in today already walks tomorrow."
- Edmund Burke: "You cannot plan the future by the past."
- Jean de La Bruyere: "Children enjoy the present because they have neither a past nor a future."

Children exemplify the concept of being. They are right in the moment, dealing with the now. Part of their innocence is wanting instant gratification. For them the future is too abstract and what is past is gone, not to be recalled again until they are in therapy as adults!

To be or not to be, that is the question I ask you. Do you want to live in the moment or dwell in the past? Do you want to be in the now or hope the future will bring better things? The decision is yours. As for me, I take life moment by moment.

I am, therefore I *am*.

A Happy Funeral?

"You can make your funeral a pleasant experience…" read the advertisement in my local paper. For whom, I wonder. Certainly not for me. I'll be stone cold, no longer able to use my wit to liven things up.

I don't feel death is ever a laughing matter. There was a tasteless film about a few friends who drag a corpse around. It was billed as a comedy, but it was in the poorest taste imaginable. Anyone who has lost a loved one knows there is nothing funny about it.

Do you fear dying? If so you are not alone. Most of us have anxieties about passing from this world.

"The more complete one's life is, the more one's creative capacities are fulfilled, the less one fears death," writes Lisl Marburg Goodman. "People are not afraid of death per se, but of the incompleteness of their lives."

I believe that is true. Think of all the things you plan to do somewhere down the road. Now is the time to do them—for there may not be a tomorrow.

If you were to die today, would you have any regrets?

"Once you accept your own death all of a sudden you are free to live," says Saul Alinsky. "You no longer care about your reputation, you no longer care except so far as your life can be used tactically—to promote a cause you believe in."

If we act as though today were our last day on Earth, there would be kinder and gentler words going round. Most people don't want to think nobody will attend their funeral. They don't want to be remembered for being a tyrant—even if they are.

If you have a boss who yells and screams and he knew that tomorrow was his last day here, don't you think there would be a quick attitude adjustment? I'll bet there would.

The Irish wake is a gleeful time—maybe that's what is meant by a happy funeral. Although the departed will be missed, George Bernard Shaw has these wise words:

"Life does not cease to be funny when people die any more than it ceases to be serious when people laugh."

Satisfaction Guaranteed

I received a brochure in the mail that read, "How to Communicate with Confidence, Clarity and Credibility." The price was $79.99—Satisfaction Guaranteed!

The material is designed to entice business people to spend their money on a one-day workshop that will boost their professional effectiveness. The brochure explained that no less than 58 separate topics would be covered between 9 a.m. and 4 p.m. (minus one hour and a half for lunch and bathroom breaks).

Calculating in my head, I figure the speakers have 330 minutes of actual training time, meaning they give each topic a full five minutes and 42 seconds—*satisfaction guaranteed!*

I have spent most of my life dealing with communication. It is something we all must work on daily, not just for 330 minutes in a oneday seminar. And yet they claim satisfaction is guaranteed.

Too many seminars in this business of self-help concentrate on "how to" instead of "helping me want to." Motivation is the key. A person can know all the facts, but if the drive is missing, nothing will happen.

So let me give this word of caution. If you get a brochure in the mail that offers a workshop or seminar with satisfaction guaranteed, be wary before plunking down your money. Find out exactly how they will approach the topic—whether it is a true motivational technique or a lecture telling you how to, but offering no concrete formulas for improvement.

Ancient Truths

From the *Bhagavad Gita,* a beautiful and inspiring book from ancient India, comes this thought written more than 2,000 years ago: "Better one's own duty, though imperfect, than another's duty well performed."

And from Greece, this axiom written by Polybius at about the same time: "There is no witness so dreadful, no accuser so terrible as the conscience that dwells in the heart of every man."

Whenever I work with people, the above truths constantly come up. They may be old, but they'll never be antiques. Seems as though people will do almost anything except find out who they really are. They are content to get by in life without making so much as a ripple. They react, instead of proact—which takes some thinking.

Some philosophers claim we are locked into one of three positions: life's watchers, doers and the totally ignorant. Some of us are lucky enough to go through all stages in one lifetime.

I started out as ignorant of anything outside the all-important ME. I then moved on to being an observer. Finally, I decided to participate in the human experience. One thing is for certain, it keeps life from being dull.

Learning to use the you, instead of always using me, connects me to the universe (with you).

Reading ancient philosophies makes one probe and question the meaning of life—makes a person want to interact with others to see if the ancient axioms are true. It can be like conversing with the greatest minds of the past and present.

To end this week, I'd like to leave you with this ancient Chinese proverb that is one of the wisest truisms:

"Be not afraid of growing slowly; be afraid only of standing still."

"A man must not swallow more beliefs than he can digest."

BROOKS ADAMS

"Diplomacy: the art of jumping into troubled waters without making a splash."

ART LINKLETTER

Bias

A man whose ax was missing suspected his neighbor's son. The boy walked like a thief, looked like a thief and spoke like a thief.

But the man found his ax where he left it the last time he was digging, in a nearby field. The next time he saw this neighbor's son, the boy walked, talked and spoke like any other child.

This story is attributed to the philosopher Lao-tzu but the point is well taken.

Bias is a prejudiced outlook. This malady is passed from parent to child, down the line for generations. The disease usually infects children before the age of three.

The popular author/doctor, Burton White, writes: "I believe that not more than one child in 10 gets off to as good a start as he could." That means the odds are 9:1 against growing up unbiased.

Too often we lump together people of a certain race, religion or national origin instead of treating them as individuals. As a collective group, we taint them with our own preconditioned opinions.

Like sheep, most of us tend to be followers. If the people in your circle of friends belong to the KKK, chances are you will also. Unfortunately for world peace, hate is alive and well as many of our students are demonstrating. Just today there was an article in the paper on two white college boys suspended for accosting a black student. There was no rational reason for their abhorrent behavior. Did they think they were being funny, or cute, or are they just plain stupid?

Now they must accept their fate—suspension, probation, community service, an apology and a fine. They got off light as far as I am concerned.

Let us give people who were not made in our image the benefit of the doubt. If their skin is darker or lighter, if they have curly hair or straight, if they speak with an accent or worship in a different church, let us be tolerant, as we would want them to be tolerant of us.

To eradicate this terrible malady, we must make an effort to be accepting and loving, even if it means overcoming our own ingrained prejudices. It's hard work, but it will lead to a more harmonious world.

Amazing Americans

A popular magazine dedicated a recent issue to what they called "Amazing Americans." Included were the achievers, the heroes, the underdogs, and those courageous people who beat the odds with brains, luck and faith.

Here are a few:

- A California farmer raised a 500-pound pumpkin.
- A 12-year-old child climbed the tallest mountain in this country, Mt. McKinley.
- A 61-year-old man became an attorney after failing the bar exam 47 times in 25 years!
- A baby was born prematurely weighing 9.9 ounces (that's not even a pound) and survived. He is now a spunky child of two.
- A sky diver jumped from the plane and both parachutes failed to open. She fell 10,500 feet and survived.
- An 82-year-old inventor/farmer has never paid an electric bill on his 100-acre farm. He is totally energy sufficient.

All of us have inherited the same "will to win" at birth. We all have the ability to tap into the vast reservoir of human potential. Yet most of us go through life dipping in with a teaspoon when we could be using a ladle.

The people mentioned above would probably all agree that the two most important qualities they developed as children were a positive mental attitude and the will to succeed. Combine those with persistence and you have the trio that triumphs over any adversity. It's the stuff that makes heroes out of ordinary people and survivors when there are disasters.

We all have what it takes. Don't forget that the next time adversity knocks on your door.

Left and Right

As you may have noticed I allude often to the left and right hemispheres of the brain. The reason is to impress upon you the importance of understanding the basic functions of the bicameral brain. Only then can people learn to make full use of their potential, since potential leads to success. Success is defined as the proper balance between positive thinking (left side) and positive feeling (right side).

Unless we work the two halves of our brain together, we are actually fighting ourselves, working at a disadvantage. That sets up what is commonly known as a self-defeating situation where the right and left side of our brains are fighting for control, thus frustrating your efforts at gaining peace of mind. Makes sense, doesn't it?

A study made by the Sociology Department at Duke University dealt with peace of mind. Their conclusion was that most unhappiness stems from a morbid preoccupation with past mistakes and failures. This means we are using our feeling side to bring back negative emotions without the rational side erasing these negative events.

Whole brain experiences are what we must strive for.

The advertising people for a European luxury car used this concept when they ran a two-page ad designed to appeal to the thinkers and the feelers. One ad was titled "a car for the left side of your brain." It appeared on the left side and was filled with copy designed for the rational and analytical reader.

The right-hand page simply said "a car for the right side of your brain" and showed a Saab, leaving the rest to the reader's imagination.

My best description of left brain and right brain domination is to visualize two people in front of two bowls of alphabet soup. The left-brainer will eat the letters alphabetically. The right-brainer will eat the same letters by making up words on the spot.

No matter which side you tend to favor, try dipping into the opposite side. The results will surprise you and bring new dimensions to your living. The outcome? Peace of mind.

Fear

This is the Devil's day—Halloween—when ghosts and goblins roam the streets. It's a good time to talk about fear.

- Fear is faith turned inside out.
- The only thing we have to fear is fear itself.
- The fear of life is the favorite disease of the 20th century.
- There is perhaps nothing so bad and so dangerous in life as fear.

Wouldn't it be nice if we could all live without fear? If children could grow up in a world that was safe and clean and there were no bad people. Unfortunately, that's not the way it is.

We must teach youngsters from an early age that strangers are to be avoided—that nobody, not even family members—can be fully trusted. It's sad, really, that we have sunk so low that when a father, uncle or grandpa asks a child to sit on his lap, he may be suspect.

As we grow older, the fears multiply: We fear others, our own insecurities, our inferiority. Fear paralyzes the creative spark and interferes with the development of our talents and abilities. Fear turns to anger, frustration and eventually illness—which most of us already fear.

Twenty years ago, Halloween was a holiday to delight and spook the hearts of children and adults alike. Now ugly people poison candy and put razors in apples. What kind of sick minds are these?

It seems as though fear is here to stay. There is no way around it. Trust has gone out the window along with integrity, honesty and moral righteousness. I can only hope that religion and faith are here to stay, for without them it will be one mistrustful world.

We must learn to live with fear and not let it dominate our lives—and the lives of our children. They must be taught that they can operate at their highest level while still keeping a watchful eye. Trust, which is so basic to love, must always be cherished.

Let us be careful when we caution growing minds. We want them to develop with a healthy attitude but we must make them aware of the dangers without stifling their actions.

So go, enjoy your trick or treating. Play a trick on the Devil and show no fear.

*Thank God,
Praise
Yourself*

Marathon

This Sunday is the New York Marathon. This past year 25,000 people participated. It's an endurance test for the healthiest of human specimens.

I feel as though I have been on a marathon of my own—writing these vignettes for the past 11 months. I hope they are helping you gain some insight into yourself—how you think and how you can improve your life. If so, I feel gratified already.

Finding topics to write about is not hard. Lessons are all around us—at the bagel shop, at the customer service counter, at the doctor's office, even walking down the street usually leads to a chance encounter that generates a story.

Life itself is a marathon—a never-ending array of experiences and situations that make us face our shortcomings and display our strengths. We never know what is coming next, so we must always be on our toes, ready to spring into action at a moment's notice.

In high school I ran track but because my stride was short I never won any races. As I've matured, I have turned the sprinting into walking, a slow and steady pace I find comfortable and comforting. This tempo suits me, allowing me to move with ease.

How about you? Do you feel as though you are racing through a marathon, just trying to get to the finish line before anyone else? If you do, you have my deepest sympathy.

Slow down. Take time to enjoy a movie or a museum or a self-help tape. The end will be reached soon enough. What's the rush?

Or are you the opposite—sitting in your chair week after week, year after year, arteries clogging from lack of exercise?

Get up and go for a stroll. The weather should be just right for a whiff of fresh air. Make it a habit to walk every day, before work, after work or at lunch hour. It will help your mental attitude and make your body healthier. What have you got to lose?

As for marathons, I admire the men and women who push their bodies to the limit for this cruel endurance test. As far as I'm concerned, anyone who crosses the finish line is a winner.

"A good scare is worth more to a man than good advice."

ED HOWE

"There is no cure for birth or death save to enjoy the interval."

GEORGE SANTAYANA

Laughter

"When the first baby laughed for the first time, the laugh broke into a thousand pieces and they all went skipping about." J. M. Barrie, author of *Peter Pan,* wrote that lovely quote.

Laughter in children has not changed since the beginning of time, but it is becoming an increasing rarity in adults. The latest reports indicate that very young children laugh 500 times per day. As they grow, that figure diminishes to a trifling 15 laughs per day.

I wonder why that is, don't you? Laughter has been proven an antidote to illness and a stress-reliever. It would be wonderful if we could cast off some of the guilt and hangups we all carry around and recapture the innocence of youth—when we could laugh and not worry what people thought of us.

Here are some quips on laughter that may help:

- Will Rogers: "We are all here for a spell, get all the good laughs you can."
- Max Beerbohm: "Nobody ever died of laughter."
- William Thackeray: "A good laugh is sunshine in a house."
- Ed Howe: "If you don't learn to laugh at trouble, you won't have anything to laugh at when you grow old."

The trick to letting loose with a laugh is to *accept yourself.* That way you don't have to worry if anyone is laughing at you, since you'll be laughing right along with them.

Laugh and the world laughs with you. See how many laughs you can manage between today and tomorrow. Start counting.

GOD

Those are the letters painted on several trucks I've seen along the Long Island highways. No, they don't stand for God, they're an acronym for Guaranteed Overnight Delivery. Many people pray to God for instant delivery from their problems, but the Lord doesn't usually work that fast. Disappointment and lack of faith follow.

What is not understood is that there are universal laws that govern us all, and neither prayer no begging will change the way in which things work. The trick is to learn to operate within those laws and use them to your advantage.

I have found that my life runs more smoothly when I let the universe run itself without interference from me. The more I let things flow, without pushing, pulling or whining, the better it is.

There is no guaranteed overnight delivery from one's problems. Difficulties sort themselves out given time.

When confronted by a dilemma, first ask yourself if there is some remedy that you are capable of putting into action that will make it better. For instance, if you have been fired or "downsized" as they now call it, a job will not automatically come to you. You must make the effort to find one. Eventually, you will resolve the situation. Making yourself crazy over it only adds more stress.

Conversely, there are illnesses, like the flu, that simply must run their course. There is nothing you can do. Getting all worked up, thinking you can stop the virus will only keep you in bed longer. Relax, sleep, take your medicine and go with it.

As you can see God takes care of all things in time. Just remember, nobody is on *your* time schedule, especially God.

No guaranteed overnight deliveries!

Love Yourself

"When a person falls in love with himself, it's the beginning of a lifelong romance," quipped Leo Buscaglia. He has a point.

It's a well-known fact that we cannot give to others what we don't have. How can a pauper give away millions? He can't. So, too, a person who does not love him or herself cannot possibly give true love to others. It's simply not feasible.

"Love conquers all" is not a platitude. It's a law of nature. In holistic health it is recognized as the greatest healing force we can muster against catastrophic illness. Only by having the mind and body working together (synergy) can the spirit dominate.

Medical textbooks are filled with cases of amazing healings—cures that even the most astute doctors are unable to explain. Why? Because the mind is a powerful tool. The love of oneself and the domination of the will to survive can defy the laws of nature as we know them.

Mae West may have been kidding when she said: "I never loved another person the way I loved myself." But there's a certain truth to that wise woman's words.

Psychobabble

An office motto reads:

Little minds talk about people.
Ordinary minds talk about events.
Great minds talk about ideas.

I consider the first two psychobabblers since discussions of people and events usually involve the *past*. Ideas project the present into the future. That's a more profitable way to spend one's time.

Today, more than ever, I hear discussions about the attempts of people to cope with daily frustrations. We live at a frantic pace. The names of the new systems designed to make our daily routine easier are mind-boggling: psychocybernetics, transpersonal relations, bioenergetics, rolfing, rational-emotive techniques. And that doesn't include fire walking and beating drums!

Therapists are becoming a large part of the nation's $700 billion health bill. And yet the results of this self-nurturing appear to have little effect on the average American.

As Hillel the Elder (70 B.C. to 10 A.D.) said so astutely: "If I am not for myself who is for me? And being for my own self, what am I?"

I certainly believe in self-help, with the accent on self. Nobody can undo what we have done to ourselves. Each of us must do that individually. To accomplish this we must learn to release ourselves from the external stimuli that keep us occupied day and night and look into ourselves. Meditation is a wonderful tool for getting in touch with one's inner self—for unlocking the free spirit that dwells in each of us.

Once you let go of the ego trip, life takes on a new meaning. Instead of emotional immaturity, love and harmony will surface and take over. You will release the past and live in the present, which will propel you into the future with eyes and heart wide open and ready for action.

Neighbors

There are neighbors and there are neighbors. Some are positive, friendly people that we'd like to know better. Others are aloof and contrary, always finding fault. We try to steer clear of those.

In my younger years I moved around quite a bit. I always found my neighbors to be of very poor quality—socially speaking. As I grew up and relocated to different areas around New York, I realized that the new people I was meeting were quite sociable and civilized. It took me a while to realize that every time I moved I took ME along. My fears, prejudices and insecurities came with the dishes and furniture, clinging to me like fleas on a dog.

This means that in order to effect a neighborly spirit, *I* had to do some initial changing. As I altered my personality, my associates began to react to me more favorably.

Today I greet many new people with my improved attitude of positive expectancy. Those old adages of "Expect the worst and you won't be disappointed," and "As you sow, so shall you reap" now make sense. I did not see the connection between my sowing friendly seeds and my reaping the benefits of trusting relationships. These days I always expect bumper crops.

The weekend is upon us and this is an excellent time to see what kind of neighbor you are. Look closely at the people who surround you. If they treat you negatively (or if they ignore you altogether) are they mirroring your attitude? Conversely, if they are friendly and outgoing, are they reacting to you in a positive way?

Try an experiment. Make a gesture to one of your neighbors whom you have never spoken to. Introduce yourself. Offer to help with a chore, bring over a pie, stop by for a chat. See how they react. Who knows, you might be making a new best friend.

*"If you're not allowed to laugh in heaven, I don't
want to go there."*

MARTIN LUTHER

*"Love doesn't make the world go 'round. Love is
what makes the ride worthwhile."*

FRANKLIN P. JONES

"Hate the sin and love the sinner."

MAHATMA GANDHI

When More Is Less

Kids are in distress. The depressing results of a survey in the journal *Science* indicates the following:

- American children are fatter; 27 percent are obese.
- American children are more suicidal; 11.3 per 100,000.
- American children are more likely to be killed; 11.7 per 100,000.
- More than 14 percent of American children live in single-parent households.

These *mores* are definitely *less*.

The day after these dreary statistics were published I went to the store to get batteries. There were none to be had. The owner said the kids were off for Veteran's Day and had cleaned him out. They had Walkmans and Game Boys that needed charging. Meanwhile the National Council on Fitness tells us that 50 percent of the children in America are physically unfit.

Instead of pushing, pulling, moving, lifting, running, jumping, exercising and building things, they use their index finger to push a button. Presto.

Physical fitness is closely related to mental fitness. The mind and body are connected. Young minds are not reading, they are watching television and playing video games until the muscles in their fingers are knotted with tension and their bodies are filled with aggression.

How about your kids? Where do they fall? Do they eat right and exercise regularly? Or do they spend hour after hour talking on the phone, sitting in front of the idiot box, or playing arcade games?

And while we're at it, when was the last time you took a walk with your child and had a heart-to-heart chat? Yes, I know, you're stressed, time is short, tensions run high.

Please don't let your child end up like one of the statistics above—obese, suicidal, in physical danger of being killed. Take charge, take command. Be the strong one. Children need limits. Set them now and stick to your guns.

Good luck. You'll need it!

1,000 Points of Light

I'm fully convinced that whatever your mind can conceive and your heart believes, you can achieve.

You begin each day with 1,000 points of light. As the day progresses you begin to produce negative reactions. For each one subtract 100 points from the perfect beginning score. By the time you've reached five emotional upsets you have used your quota.

For many of us this happens before leaving home in the morning! Think about your reaction to burnt toast, weak coffee, a wrinkled shirt or a ripped hem. Each one costs 100 points, depending on the way you react.

Throw in a traffic jam or worse, a flat tire or car troubles of any kind, and you can see how it goes downhill in a hurry.

Self-control is the answer. It leads to self-confidence and a brighter attitude.

Amazingly enough, a positive attitude is renewable. It's possible to wake up with a bright outlook and a new 1,000 points of light even if the day before was so terrible you ended up with a score of minus 1,000.

Positive energy rises with the sun. Every day presents new opportunities for personal growth. Every encounter can brighten your 1,000 points or diminish their number depending upon your ability to control your temper and your attitude.

Remember: When a man's temper gets the best of him, it reveals the worst of him.

Work

People-related jobs are the most stressful. These include: nurses, homemakers, lawyers, physicians, the clergy, police officers, social workers, and child-care workers. The burn-out time is a scant 18 months!

The result is that the typical American worker will end up with at least 10 jobs, each lasting approximately 3.6 years. Research has also shown that the most humanitarian jobs cause the most tension. Most workers lack people skills, including the art of communicating with peers and co-workers.

The problem is that workers take their lack of skills when they move from one job to another. Instead of sharpening their interpersonal dexterity, they figure the grass is greener elsewhere. Then they are surprised to find things are more or less the same.

There is always room to improve one's talents. It's a good way to build self-esteem and enhance your positive self. The trick is to begin *at once.* Hopefully, this book has inspired you to take stock of your assets and liabilities.

If you have been thinking of leaving your job because you cannot relate to the people around you, try taking a new tack by cultivating your positives and eliminating the negatives. Examine your motives, are you running away from something or toward a new opportunity? Are you avoiding unresolved problems?

Only you can answer these questions. Think about it before making any rash decisions. Work is work. It's up to you to make the best of it.

Respect

When asked what Americans most wanted from others, a Harris poll indicated the answer was respect. Reminds me of the old Aretha Franklin song "R-E-S-P-E-C-T," and Rodney Dangerfield's gag line, "I don't get no respect."

Here's my question: Can you respect others if you don't respect yourself?

Just as it's impossible to love others without self-love, it is impossible to respect others if you feel inferior.

On a scale of one to 10, what is your respect score? If it's below 10 you are suffering from a disease you don't really have. Lack of selfrespect is a mental condition which can be turned around. Change your thinking, change your life.

As you begin to think via introspection, you'll find the answers to many questions dealing with your purpose here on Earth. Recognize your special role. Begin a new set of positive affirmations.

Repeat the mantra: *I respect me.* Then really believe it, think and feel these words to be true.

Self-realization will grow daily as you replace old messages with new ones—those designed to return to you what was lost in childhood. Renew the feelings of worthiness and raw power that you felt before they were wrenched from you by well-meaning adults.

Show yourself the proper respect you deserve.

I Go, Therefore I Am

Ever hear the old joke, "I shop, therefore I am." There's a ring of truth to that. Everywhere we go, we take ourselves along for the ride.

Years ago I made friends with myself since I was spending so much time with me.

In order to make peace between what I wanted and what I felt I deserved, I had to match my thoughts with my feelings. I formed a permanent alliance between the two warring factions. And it works.

To illustrate: I was browsing the large health shop in my neighborhood, watching people mesmerized by the plethora of color and variety of products. I noted several aisles filled with "miracle drugs" designed to alleviate the discomforts of colds, coughs and various conditions. There were hundreds of promises on those boxes. If the store depended on me to keep them in business they'd go bankrupt.

I shop, therefore I am, has no meaning for me. I know what I want and need. Do you? Or do you think that buying something will make you happy? I hate to burst your bubble, but a new object only provides temporary relief. The problem will still be there even after the bill has been paid.

Rational thinking takes hard work and introspection. Every night before I go to sleep I wade through the clutter in my mind trying to sort out what I think and feel. I sort through the junk and accept some points as being valid and requiring more thought. Others I toss into the mental trash, to be forgotten forever with a good night's sleep.

This method keeps me out of the stores and keeps me from spending my hard-earned money on useless items I really don't need.

Are you heading for the mall tomorrow? If so, tonight before going to bed, think about what you are planning to buy.

- Is it something you need?
- Is it something you desire?
- Is it something you hope will bring a bit of happiness into your dreary life?

If it's the second or third, go to the park or the movies instead and save yourself a bunch of money. Have a good weekend.

"Remember that when you're in the right you can afford to keep your temper, and when you're in the wrong you can't afford to lose it."

MAHATMA GANDHI

*"Yesterday is a canceled check.
Tomorrow is a promissory note.
Only today is legal tender.
Only this moment is negotiable."*

AVETT ROBERT

Power Words

Recently I gave a two-hour lecture at the Center for Successful Living on Long Island. I asked the attendees about the need to *feel important*. Nine out of 10 felt it was the number one emotional need. This is fully in line with psychologists who maintain that 93 percent of what we say and do is designed to make us feel more important.

Assuming this is the case, motivating others becomes easy: just make them feel important and they'll reach new heights. Even in everyday language, the use of positive-oriented words can help improve the self-esteem of your spouse, children, co-workers, friends and peers. Here are a few words you already know. Try using them:

Adorable, beautiful, better, competent, creative, delightful, desirable, excellent, fun, gracious, generous, good, honorable, imaginative, insightful, joyous, keen, kind, lovable, multi-faceted, nice, neat, optimistic, perfect, precise, quick-witted, quaint, respectful, sincere, talented, unique, valuable, wonderful, wise, extraordinary, you're welcome, zesty.

These power words, if used daily and directed toward others, will multiply themselves tenfold in favorable reactions.

Develop a mental red flag when using negative words. Learn to switch them in midair for positive ones whenever you speak.

Intalk

Intalk is one of my original words. I think it complements words like insight, intuition, inspiration, since they all represent a capacity which manifests itself from the inside out.

Intalk takes place within the brain. We all do it when the left side argues or debates with the right—when the rational and the reasoning parts of us are at odds.

We rarely "intalk" when everything is fine. Imagine a conversation that goes like this:

"How are you feeling today, Right Brain?"

"Just fine, Lefty, and you?"

No, that's not the way it goes. Intalk usually goes more like this:

"I want that new car, Lefty, and nothing you can say will stop me from buying it."

"Don't be ridiculous, Right Brain, you can't afford it."

"I don't care, Lefty, I want what I want. You can't tell me what to do."

This three-pound slab of gray matter that we carry around in a protective casing on our neck gives us more trouble than anything external. The arguments that rage within can be ferocious; the negative energy stimulated can make us catatonic—unable to function; our thinking process can make us physically ill.

Most of our intalk is garbage. So just as I asked you to filter out negatives when you talk, try it with your intalk as well.

Prosperity

"How to Develop a Prosperity Consciousness During Difficult Times" is a lecture I have given many times. Before the session begins I like to wander around the conference room listening to peoples' view on business. This gives me a handle on the group's collective attitude so I can personalize my talk to meet their specific needs. Generally speaking, most groups are *problem-oriented* and the room usually echoes with negative feelings, or to be more specific, lack of enthusiasm for their work.

When the zeal is gone, we turn into zombies.

The general consensus of most groups I lecture to is that the boss wants more work from the workers without any raise in pay, perks or incentives. No wonder so many employees think of their bosses as SOBs.

Taking the boss's viewpoint for a minute, I'd like to point out that if it's true we only work at 2 percent of our potential, what's wrong with asking a worker to do more?

Prosperity means economic well-being. Enthusiasm is emotional well-being as well as the catalyst to prosperity. The vibrations from enthusiastic workers travel like ripples in a pond when a pebble is dropped in. Likewise, enthusiasm and a few perks from a boss go a long way in reviving sagging zest and zeal. A small bonus or an extra hour off inspires. It also shows inspired leadership. Like the kind words listed on Monday, kindness pays off in kind.

Then you've got a true win-win scenario.

Polarity and Synergy

Synergy: working together.
Polarity: remaining antagonists.

We are all born with the thinking and feeling sides of our brain as friends. Yet in my travels I tested 5,733 men and women who attended my lectures and guess what I found?

- 5,123 use their feeling mode almost exclusively.
- Only 610 were thinking their way through life.

That tells me that almost 90 percent of us *act first* and think later. We buy because we like it, then we go home and rationalize why we needed to spend the money. The explanations get more elaborate as the cost of the purchase increases.

Conversely, if we go shopping for something we truly need, then rationalize why we can't get it because of the money, we also have a problem.

The answer is to consciously cross over from one side of the brain to the other, thus creating a fertile environment for a logical discussion of the pros and cons. We've discussed this issue before—the thinking left brain and the emotional right brain, but it bears repeating.

There must be a balance. And in many cases, you've got to learn to let go of something you want or need because there is no agreement internally.

The key to synergy is compromise—not only within yourself, but with other people. We haven't really touched on this topic but we will next week.

Responsibility

An article in the paper inspired this vignette. The headline in bold reads "Parents of teen crushed by soda machine file suit."

A 13-year-old boy was killed in Florida when a 1,200-pound soft drink machine toppled over on him. How is that possible? Then I read on.

The boy had put his foot in the soda dispensing chute, pulled himself up, put his hands on top of the vending machine and began rocking. When the machine toppled, he found his foot had become wedged in the opening and he couldn't jump clear. The results were tragic.

The parents are suing the vending machine company, the store where it was located (for not bolting it down) and the mall owners (for having a sidewalk that was not level).

While I grieve for a young life cut short and I grieve for the parents who have lost their son, I also wonder about the wisdom of the young lad. Who is to assume the ultimate responsibility?

Kids will be kids, but that was a pretty stupid thing to do. What did he hope to accomplish? Did he want a soda but didn't have the money to pay for it? That would be stealing. Did he insert his coins and get no satisfaction? That's what store managers are for. Or did he just not think?

Responsibility is a huge issue. We are all accountable for our own actions. Nobody else is. Every time you get in your car and do something foolish, you must assume control for the risks you take. Every time you let your children play with something dangerous, you are accountable.

As kids grow, they slowly assume their own liability. It is up to you to teach them well and set good examples. Do as I do, not as I say.

Accidents happen. But more often than not, someone is to blame. Remember this vignette. It could save your life, or the life of someone you love.

"The deepest principle of human nature is the craving to be appreciated."

WILLIAM JAMES

"One of the saddest experiences which can come to a human being is to awaken, gray-haired and wrinkled, near the close of an unproductive career, to the fact that all through the years he has been using only a small part of himself."

V. W. BURROWS

College Chaos

Not long ago I addressed 200 college students. My topic was "Power Selling for the 90s." I thought I could motivate these young adults to choose a career in marketing and sales.

As I looked at the textbook they used, I could easily see why they might need a healthy dose of motivation. It was dry, boring, dull. Judging by the intelligent questions they posed after I had finished speaking, these bright students seemed way ahead of the material.

What I explained was that selling depends on the proper approach to buyers, who are first and foremost *people*. Most purchases are emotional, so the appeal must be made with heartfelt perks. They can be free and are very cost-effective. Knowing how to stroke the client's ego is crucial to marketing success.

I asked them to put themselves in the customer's shoes and to react to these concepts:

- Appreciation
- Praise
- Respect
- Empowerment
- Attention
- Reassurance
- Acceptance

All of these are effective tools in making a sale or getting a point across. If someone is praising, respecting, and accepting you, chances are you'll listen to what is being said.

Unfortunately, colleges today do not stress the people side of learning. It's as though institutions of higher learning are just factories which take the students' money (and lots of it), then chug them out on an assembly line. Now and then a pupil is lucky enough to have a professor who makes a difference, but they are becoming a rare commodity.

Fortunately for me, only two of the students left the lecture giving me a 99 percent success rate. That's a pretty good ratio these days.

Sacred and Profane

As we approach the holidays, I begin to hear more profane language. Is it my imagination, or are people cursing more? Tempers flare and patience is in short supply as the buying frenzy begins in earnest.

And I ask, how can someone buy a gift for a loved one when they are so consumed with anger? This is a time of thanks, of peace on Earth, good will toward men (and women). Yet I constantly hear "jerk," "idiot," "moron," bandied about—even from children. So many people seem to have a chip on their shoulder. That's a lot of lumber out there.

Those of us looking for a better self-image should get off the self-destruct wagon right now. We must make it our business to ditch the profane and spend more time cultivating our sacred side.

Sacred: blessed, divine, entitled to respect.

We are all of these things, each and every one of us. We are entitled to respect. Likewise, we should all be showing those qualities to others, for it will boomerang back to us if we don't.

Self-respect and respect for others are the springboards for human communication. And I say to you, don't just wait for the holidays to change your attitude. Carry these positive feelings around winter, spring, summer and fall. Do unto others…

As the saying goes: Gentleness is a divine trait; nothing is so strong as gentleness and nothing is so gentle as real strength.

Turkey Day

Are you ready for Turkey Day?

Do you have the bird thawing, the cranberry sauce chilling, the pies baking, the stuffing mixed, the potatoes ready and waiting?

Thanksgiving is one of my favorite holidays. It is a time to give thanks for what we have. It is the most positive day of the year. There are no negatives on Thanksgiving, unless you eat too much and make yourself sick, or take pictures of the event.

Family and friends gather in an atmosphere of ambiance and good cheer to watch the football games and eat wonderful foods, blessing God for their bounty. And while you are busy handing out the benedictions, don't forget to include yourself. For without your hard work and diligence, the day would be less than perfect.

As the day progresses, the house fills with the aromas that make my mouth water. And I thank my father for saving us from the Nazis and getting us out of Europe. I thank my mother for her caring and her wisdom, and I thank my wife, Carole, for her love.

Look around at those you wish to thank and don't be afraid to say "thanks" to those you love—and even those you don't. A little charity goes a long way.

Giving Thanks

It's here! My favorite day.

I promise I won't eat more than my share, and that I'll help with the preparation, and the cleaning up. I promise to pay attention to everyone and not get carried away with the ball game. I promise to say a prayer of thanks to God and to everyone else in the universe who has helped me celebrate this day.

I know this is a busy day for everyone so I'll make it short.

Say a prayer today for everything good that is in your life. Take stock of all the positives:

- Your health (even if you've got aches and pains)
- Your job (even if it isn't the best)
- Your family (even if they give you a bit of grief)
- Your friends (even if they burden you with their problems)
- Your co-workers (even if you don't always agree)
- Your boss (even if he didn't give you a raise)

There are so many wonderful facets to our lives. Let us spend the day dwelling on them. Set aside a day without one negative thought (even if the turkey comes out dry and the potatoes are lumpy).

And remember, when you sit down to eat, Goethe's wise words: "Out of moderation a pure happiness springs."

Amen.

Batteries Not Included

Here we go, the Christmas rush is on. Today it begins.

The shelves of the toy stores are stocked high with bright packages. What do they contain?

Terminator 2 Mobile Assault Vehicles, Pit-fighter planes, Bonk's Revenge, Mercenary Force, Air Force-22 Interceptor missiles, guns, swords, hatchets—tools of doom and destruction.

This is what we are teaching our children: It is okay to harm and even to kill others. That's quite a message as we enter the time of peace on Earth, good will toward all.

Every time we put a weapon—yes, even fake ones—into the hands of young impressionable children, we are saying loud and clear "Violence is acceptable."

The reality is brutality is not acceptable, not in a civilized world. Violence has not solved anything. It never will.

You might say that my aversion to these toys comes from my childhood. I grew up during World War II. But that's not the only reason.

Children must be taught to use their brain, not their brawn to solve their problems. Sure, if a boss doesn't give you a raise you can slug him. See where that gets you.

These days we are already seeing the long-term effects of these violent toys—disgruntled workers bringing assault weapons to the workplace and opening fire. Don't you see the connection? Can you honestly say that little Johnny playing with a gun when he is seven or eight has nothing to do with his behavior as a grownup? That's a pretty big assumption. What if you are wrong?

The shelves of the toy store are also lined with fun things that challenge the thought process. Those are the games that give a solid foundation for the rest of one's life.

Do yourself a favor and do your kids a service when you pick out holiday gifts. Think about what is good for your child, not simply what he or she has been craving. In the long run, you'll both be winners.

"What another would have done as well as you,
do not do it.
What another would have said as well as you,
do not say it.
What another would have written as well as you,
do not write it.
Be faithful to that which exists nowhere but
in yourself.
And, thus, make yourself indispensable."

ANDRÉ GIDE

"Everything in excess is opposed to nature."

HIPPOCRATES

*Gifts from
the Heart*

Life's a Bitch

I was driving home from a successful lecture when I spotted a bumper sticker on the car in front of me that read: "Life's a bitch and so am I!"

The driver was young and attractive which made me wonder what made her decide to advertise—and thus fulfill—a very negative outlook on life at such a tender age. I can practically guarantee she'll get out of life exactly what she programmed in via her bumper sticker.

Life can only be life. It can't be a bitch. The bitch part is what a person brings to it. A dash of hatred, two shakes of anger, a teaspoon of fear, a tablespoon of anxiety, a cup of sorrow and you have a recipe for suffering.

The bumper sticker should read: "I am a bitch, therefore life is also a bitch."

I cannot get into this young woman's mind to find out what caused this mental self-abuse but I know for a fact that she could change her adverse condition—first to neutral, then to constructive thinking. The will to win triumphs over life's adversities.

Just as a recipe is the product of the ingredients, what we get out of life is a product of what we put into it. The young woman driving the car with the bitch bumper sticker needs to change the recipe she is cooking up if she doesn't want to end up a bitter and stale old maid. Right now she is programming in what she thinks she wants. The tragedy is she will probably get it.

As Oscar Wilde said in his classic work *Portrait of Dorian Gray*:

"In this world there are only two tragedies: One is not getting what one wants, the other is getting it."

Nothing and Everything

You and I are nothing and yet we are everything. Here are some startling facts about us:

- Each one of the billions of atoms that makes up our bodies is 99.99 percent empty space.
- Atoms, which were once thought of as the smallest particle, are actually made up of *quanta* which are 100,000 times smaller than their host cells.
- All quanta are made up of invisible vibrations waiting to do their thing.
- Every one of the 100 trillion cells in our body contains a single strand of DNA comprised of 3,000,000,000 genetic bits.

All of those zeroes are mind-boggling. But they do point out that we are *basically nothing*—an empty space until a mind and soul are attached. On the other hand, we are everything—a miracle of thought and feeling held together by vibrating molecules!

Each of us is a miracle—a walking, talking marvel in motion. So each of us has the power to be anything we want to be. We can take the billions of atoms with their vibrating quanta and become a productive member of society, or we can let it all go to waste. Nobody can make that decision for you.

You must decide whether you want to be a nothing or an everything.

4-Fs

During World War II, 4-Fs were men and women who could not serve in the military because of physical disabilities.

Today the phrase 4-F carries a new meaning: When problems arise we must Fix them as quickly as possible so we can be Free of stress. That can usually be accomplished by Forgiveness which leads to Fulfillment.

By not deploying the 4-F method, you and the object of your anger are tied together in a psychological tug-of-war, each holding one end of the rope.

If you release your end, your adversary will fall flat and will be left holding the bag (rope), thus directing any ill feelings inward.

By letting go, you avoid getting "roped in" and, at the same time, release the negative energy. Whether you are forgiven by your enemy is not important as long as you do your best to let go of destructive feelings.

Excusing others is far better than *accusing* them. So mind your Ps and Qs and keep the 4-Fs in mind:

To Fix your problems, Forgive others, Free yourself of stress and find Fulfillment.

Planned Obsolescence

Manufacturers rejoice in it.
Retailers pray for it.
Customers cringe at it.

Did you know that products have been manufactured that are indestructible? In fact, I have a pair of socks invented a number of years ago made of a miracle fiber called Vibram. They have been washed at least 500 times (and worn just as many). They look as good now as when they were bought. They will probably be around long after I am gone.

The human body was designed by God to last a maximum of about 120 years. When centenarians are interviewed they are usually still full of vim and vigor (maybe they have the miracle fiber Vibram woven into their molecules!).

Why, then do so many of us think that we are decrepit when we pass the 60-year mark? Why do some of us think that retirement means death is just around the corner?

A job is a job, a career is just that—a career. There should be a life outside that.

Once you have time to spare, you may be surprised to find you ever had time to work at all. Talk to some retirees who volunteer or play golf, tennis or have taken up a hobby. They'll tell you life has never been so rewarding or fulfilling.

If you retire at 65 and live another 30 years, you'll need something to do with your time. That doesn't mean sitting around the house moaning about how unfair life is and how you have nothing to do.

The only planned obsolescence in the human life cycle is the one you plan for!

So take this advice and plan well. Start today.

The Ages of Mankind

Age is a state of mind, not a measure of one's abilities. There are high achievers at both ends of the age spectrum. The difference is that some seem unencumbered by the trivia that frustrates the majority of us. Here are a few examples:

- Mozart was already playing the harpsichord and violin—and performing—by age three!
- Frederic Chopin was a child prodigy, starting his career at age seven.
- Bobby Fischer became the youngest International Grand Master of chess at age 15.
- Premiere ballerina Margot Fonteyn began dancing with a much younger partner, Rudolf Nureyev, at age 42.
- Grandma Moses took up painting at age 70 and had her first one-woman exhibit at 80.
- At age 75 Ed Delano from California bicycled to his 50th high school reunion—a distance of 3,100 miles!
- At age 81, Benjamin Franklin mediated the convention of delegates so the Constitution of the United States could be adopted.
- At age 84 Winston Churchill won a parliamentary election.
- George Selbach of Michigan scored a hole-in-one at age 96 and is still playing golf at age 98.
- At age 106 Marjory Stoneman Douglas is still crusading for the restoration of the Everglades in Florida!

One of the common threads that runs through each of these achievers is purpose. They all have a reason—above and beyond the norm—to excel. They are inner-directed. Their enthusiasm is undimmed by external happenings.

Why alibi yourself into early senility? Forget chronological age and concentrate on doing your best, at any age.

"Inventing is a combination of brains and materials. The more brains you use, the less material you need."

CHARLES F. KETTERING

"A good man makes no noise over a good deed, but passes on to another as a vine to bear grapes again in season."

MARCUS AURELIUS

"I'm not interested in age. People who tell their age are silly. You're as old as you feel."

ELIZABETH ARDEN

Death Grip

I was seated in a hotel lobby one Sunday morning waiting for a taxi to take me to the airport. Nearby, within earshot, were two children, their mother and father, an aunt and an uncle. They were attending the funeral of the mother's father—the children's grandfather.

Since he had been asked to say something nice about his father-inlaw, the husband turned to the wife and asked for some information about the deceased. What I heard chilled my blood.

The entire conversation revolved around the father's abuse of his daughters. He alternately mistreated and ignored them. He never showed love and affection. He was a terrible husband.

The woman said she had forgiven her father for his offenses, but her body language betrayed her words. She was obviously still in great pain over the rejection she suffered as a child.

This woman was in a death grip. The old man had her in his power, even though he was no longer alive. Although I knew I was eavesdropping, I could not help myself as I watched them struggle for something positive to say. Inside I ached for the grandchildren who had to listen to these terribly negative things being said about their grandpa. It will no doubt guarantee mental and physical problems in the future. The mother and her sister are still suffering.

There is a lesson here and it is two-fold. The first is that we must learn to forgive, *really* forgive. Holistic health demands we get rid of the harmful past. Only then can the natural order of things take place without interference from our minds. This includes pardoning ourselves, removing the guilt that was installed in us before we could understand what was happening.

The second lesson is for the dead man—and those like him who are still among us. Atone now while you still have time. Think for a moment what will be said about you at your funeral. Will people be glad to see you go? Will they find anything good to say? Or will they sincerely mourn your parting? What will they put on your tombstone?

You can do something about it now. It's never too late to change.

Peeping Toms

We are all mental peeping Toms to some degree. I don't mean we look in other people's windows. Instead we peep into their minds, wondering what they will think about us. The fact that so many of us worry about the opinions of our neighbors and others, proves that we carry on a lot of needless mental activity.

Your opinions must come first. If you can please others without losing your own sense of self, that's wonderful. If not, to your own self be true (Shakespeare).

When outside pressures try to control your behavior, it often causes mental anguish. We must all learn to follow our instincts (our gut reactions) instead of being led like a bull with a ring in its nose.

Others want us to be like them, to validate their thoughts and lifestyles. This always hits home when I see motorcycle gangs racing down the highway. They all look exactly the same. Under the black leather, the tattoos, and the protruding beer guts I know they are each unique. But they run in packs, in a strange game of follow-the-leader, obliterating their individuality. I always wonder, what if one of them decided to wear a bright pink leather jacket?

Each of us is special. We should try to retain this gift for life. Personal growth is enhanced when one sticks to one's own convictions without deliberately stepping on anyone else's needs and beliefs. Remember: to others your ideas may be wrong.

Want to know if you are your own person? Go to the mirror and look into your eyes. Say "I love and accept you just as you are." If you believe in yourself, you'll hold your own gaze. There will be no doubt or question in your mind. If you affirm positively, you will not become a slave to the ideas of others. You will have the confidence of your own conviction and you will not need to seek the approval of others.

The Pessimist and the Optimist

The pessimist was put in a room of toys and cried because there was nothing to play with. The optimist was put in a room of horse manure and waded happily through it knowing there must be a pony nearby.

A pessimist and an optimist jumped off the roof of a high building. On the way down the pessimist said: "I know I'm going to kill someone when I hit bottom." The optimist said: "So far so good!"

Actually this last scenario could not happen. An optimist doesn't give up and jump off high buildings.

Many would argue that we are born with a predisposition to be either an optimist or a pessimist. Rubbish. We can turn pessimism around to optimism with some hard work and many positive affirmations. There is no reason to see a glass half empty when it is really half full.

Pessimists allow their negative energy to color the way they see the world. They go to a party and know they'll have a bad time. They get in the car and know they'll have an accident. They go for a job interview knowing they won't get the position. They order a meal and know it will taste bad. Do you see what is happening here?

It's a simple case of self-fulfilling prophecy. What we think is what we get.

Optimists go to a party hoping to have a good time. They get in the car knowing they will arrive safely. They go for a job interview with the expectation of being hired. They order a meal knowing it will taste yummy.

Even if an optimist goes to a party and has a rotten time, gets into the car and has a blowout, doesn't get the job and has a bland meal, there's always tomorrow.

I cannot stress the importance strongly enough. What goes around comes around. Think negative thoughts and that's what you'll get—and vice versa.

But let me tell you one thing: If there is horse manure around, surely a pony *is* nearby!

George's Advice

A recent interview with George Stephanopoulos, President Clinton's senior advisor, was intriguing enough for me to include it as a vignette. For a young man of 35, he has some interesting and effective thoughts on life learned from his years as a golf caddy, congressional aide and presidential confidante.

- Give advice when asked and shut up when you're not asked.
- You can apologize for not doing your work, for not being honest or loyal. But don't apologize for working as hard as you can.
- Unhealthy intimidation makes you afraid to speak. Healthy intimidation makes you prepared.
- A little voice of doubt in the back of your mind is good, because it leads to a certain humility and tolerance for someone else's point of view.
- You have to learn to live with criticism. Sometimes you have to let attacks go. But when criticism is provably wrong, that's when you fight back.
- Don't expect the impossible. Not every problem has a simple solution.
- Look at the bright side.

Although this clever young man was fired in 1993 as the White House communications director, his insights indicate a high degree of optimism. We can all learn a lesson from George's wise words.

Attitude

Over $40 billion a year is spent annually to help people improve their *aptitude* but only a fraction of that amount is spent on improving *attitude*.

As I have been saying all along, mental attitudes can work miracles. That was proven by the Menninger Clinic in Topeka, Kansas when they interpreted 400 spontaneous remissions of cancer. The only common denominator found was a change of attitude by the patients. They broke away from the Doomsday scenario and rewrote the script with a happy ending. In spite of the dismal medical findings and prophecies, they dug deep within themselves to find a new, inexplicable strength. The choice was made to live, not die. We call it a miracle since it cannot be explained logically.

Much of my time is spent explaining how we continue to nurture negative attitudes as adults. It becomes a habit—much easier to fall back on the familiar than to try a different approach, look for alternate answers, do things another way.

Going around in circles may be natural for a wheel, but it means going backward for anyone who wants to grow. A new attitude can supplant an old one by continued exposure to it. A consistently positive vision will give new life to old thoughts.

Albert Einstein said it takes 11 positives to eliminate one negative. We can easily see our work is cut out for us.

You may not have a life-threatening disease, but you will begin to feel better immediately when you change your attitude and take full charge of your life.

"Society attacks early, when the individual is helpless."

B. F. SKINNER

"There is no sadder sight than a young pessimist."

MARK TWAIN

"Everyone is bound to assert his rights and resist their invasion by others."

IMMANUEL KANT

The G Spot

In yesterday's newspaper, Dr. Ruth proclaimed "There is no such thing as a G spot." I disagree.

There is a G spot but it has nothing to do with a woman's anatomy. We all have one. It's the place where Guilt dwells.

I say guilt is a waste of time. Think about it. What does it accomplish? Does it help you earn a better salary or be a better spouse? Are you prettier or wiser because of guilt?

If the leaders of the world's religions united their thoughts into one feeling I hope it would sound like this: "Sinner forgive yourself."

Guilt comes in handy when others want to control you. Parents, teachers, spouses, siblings, bosses, friends and lovers find the weak spot in our character then use it to dominate our spirit.

The only time guilt serves a purpose is when it is used to eliminate wrong actions toward others. If I hurt someone on purpose, guilt should make me stop the destructive behavior. When I do something negative a small voice inside my head says "You can't do that or you'll feel bad about yourself later."

Shakespeare said, "Suspicion always haunts the guilty mind." How right he is.

Dr. Max Levine said: "Guilt automatically produces fear… you can fool people, but you can't fool your own autonomic nervous system."

So there you have it, folks. The G spot is alive and well in each of us.

I have given up guilt. We all make mistakes we'd like to erase; we've all done something stupid or hurtful. The trick is not to dwell on it, to relieve yourself of the burden. Put it on the shelf or down the garbage disposal.

Sinner, forgive yourself.

The Power of Music

Paul Simon, the gifted singer, drew 750,000 people to a concert in Manhattan's Central Park. There was not one negative incident. It proved once again that America is a wonderful melting pot when it wants to be.

Of course the music helped keep everyone at peace and in tune. It was obvious that music is a great healer. And the power of the people was evident.

Since we haven't had an acronym in a while, here goes:

P: Positive *vibes*
O: Optimistic *lyrics*
W: Wholesome *ideas*
E: Enthusiastic *entertainment*
R: *Restraint*

Music transcends race, religion and national boundaries. It sweetens a sour mood, it makes the body move, it takes the mind off one's troubles as the alpha waves flow. Music blocks out pain and inspires the imagination.

Music is power and powerful music stimulates. Power to the people who listen to *good* music.

P.S. Music makes a great holiday gift: a cassette or CD, concert tickets, a musical instrument or gift certificate to a music store.

Visualize and Vitalize

In 1959 a Chinese concert pianist named Liu Chi Kung was imprisoned. Only a year before he had come in second to Van Cliburn in the Tchaikovsky piano competition.

While in prison Kung was denied the use of a musical instrument. Yet when he was released he embarked on a world tour. According to the critics, he played better than before although he had not practiced at a piano for seven years while in prison. When asked how that was possible, Kung replied that he had practiced every day—in his mind.

That is a perfect example of vitalizing a visualization.

The same technique is used by the top sports professionals. They play over the correct techniques for hitting a ball, skiing down a slalom slope, slapping a puck into the goal or sinking a putt. The muscles are trained while they sleep. They picture the positive result they want to attain and concentrate on it. When the time comes to play—*voilà*, a winner.

The idea behind visualizing is to "see" only that which you want. Great golfers "see" only the green and the hole, which is the ultimate goal. They do not concentrate on the sand traps or water holes which are negative spaces.

The same goes for any profession, especially sales. Visualize the closing, the moment of truth. Make it come true in your dreams so when the time is at hand, you will be mentally prepared.

We've already seen how this works with illness. While not every malady can be cured with positive thoughts, many of them can and are.

The father of American psychology, William James, agrees: "The greatest discovery of my generation is that human beings can alter their lives by changing their attitudes of mind."

Why Me?

In today's Ziggy cartoon he's sitting with his head in his hands. The caption above reads:

"If I had a nickel for every time I said 'why me!?' I'd probably have said 'why me!?' a lot more often."

Why do we always ask "why me?" We only ask when something bad happens. Does anyone ever say "why me?" when they win the lottery? I sincerely doubt it.

Misfortunes fall into everybody's lives. Sometimes they are small, sometimes they are huge. Sometimes they come in clumps (three is the number most associated with disasters).

An attorney I know lost in quick succession his uncle, his father and his younger sister. Then he was struck with kidney stones, his wife was in a car accident and his son's new car was stolen in New Orleans while he was celebrating Mardi Gras. "Why me?" he asked.

I've heard it said that God dishes out just as much as we can deal with. This attorney had some rough times but he dealt with it. There was nothing to do about his uncle, his father and his sister. Funeral arrangements were made, he helped his mother through her grief, he bought his son a new car, and his wife was treated and released. He counted himself lucky that things were not worse.

Did God give him too much? Yes, perhaps. Yet this man made it through his pain and is now back practicing law, playing golf, and enjoying his family. He considers himself lucky.

So once again, it's an attitude thing. Nobody will get through life without some disaster—whether large or small. There is no way to prepare except to know when things are down, they can only get better. Every cloud has a silver lining. All the corny cliches go to work when calamity befalls us.

So, like Ziggy with his nickels, be aware that there are positive lessons to be learned from every misfortune. You may not be richer but hopefully you will be wiser.

The Science of Sex

Both radio and television are blaring that there are only five shopping days left until Christmas, so I thought I'd take your mind off money and put it elsewhere.

At one time sex was a private matter between two consenting adults. Now it seems anything goes. There are even new terms like "sexperts"—people who are experts in sex. What ever happened to romance?

Over the years there have been studies and surveys to keep track of our sexual habits and preferences. There have been books and articles on sex appeal and sexuality. But a recent article in the paper lists a new glut of books that reduce what was once a passionate pastime to psychodynamics, hormones, testosterone and other biochemical factors.

It puts the fantasy part of romance on the back burner and flames the idea of the right-brain versus left-brain thinking. Hormones may point us in one direction but our head still makes the final call. Talk about thinking and feeling tugging in opposite directions—romance is the perfect example.

How do these titles grab you? The Alchemy of Love and Lust, The Hormone of Desire, Sex Appeal: Who Has It and How to Get It.

They sound intriguing but I'll take the good old-fashioned kind of sex any day. Just me and my wife together, alone, letting our hormones do their thing without wondering how it's all working.

Perhaps you can take some time this weekend to explore your own romantic side. If you have a partner, so much the better. If not, take some time to think about why it is that you are alone. Is it because you want to be? Are you negative toward sex? Or are you picky? There are plenty of people out there. Nobody is perfect so maybe there are some attitude adjustments that could be made to accommodate that fact. I don't mean you should settle or stay with someone who is abusive. Never let that happen.

I mean instead of analyzing everything to death, let the heart take over and let the science of sex take a back seat for a change (no pun intended).

Enjoy the weekend.

*"Deep within our consciousness is the realization
there is a Higher Power… our Lord and God.
That our life has a purpose, a destiny, a meaning,
a relationship which must be discovered and
developed. Until this is achieved you will experience
boredom, frustration, dissatisfaction. Only the
indwelling presence of this Power will satisfy the
hunger of your soul."*

ALFRED A. MONTAPERT

*"There is no future in any job. The future lies in
the man who holds the job."*

DR. GEORGE CRANE

*"Passions are vices or virtues in their
highest powers."*

GOETHE

Compromise

I think I promised a vignette on compromise a while back. With the holidays upon us, this is a good time to fulfill my promise.

Compromise: settlement of differences by arbitration or by consent reached by mutual concessions.

The key words here are "mutual concessions." That's where both parties give a little. It reminds me of a popular country western song with lyrics that go "I'll keep going my way and you keep going yours… we'll take a little time and we'll each give a little… and we'll meet in the middle."

Yelling, sulking, hitting or leaving never settled a problem; violent and/or passive behavior intensifies an already volatile situation. The only way to compromise (without compromising oneself) is to talk it out.

The holidays are filled with high stress. Families come together and friction is inevitable; money is short and guilt is plentiful; the weather is usually dreadful making travel plans hazardous; loneliness is ever present even in the midst of festivities. Is it any wonder that tempers flare and battles reign supreme?

Compromise can be used on every level to promote holiday cheer—from the location of the Christmas dinner to the type of presents bought and the amount of money spent.

This is a time to put into action all the things you have learned from this book during the past year: Feel good about yourself, know that you are entitled to your opinion and it is as valid as anybody else's. Get rid of the negative past. This holiday is brand new, it has never been here before, try to forget the hurts of your childhood and see the day with new eyes.

Remain positive and focused on the tasks at hand; make compromise a number-one priority.

And remember one more thing: Nobody owes you anything. If you want to give, that is your choice. Others are not under the same obligation. If you don't receive a gift from someone you have given to, try not to be hurt. The joy comes from sharing, not receiving.

Self-Love

Did you hug yourself today? If you don't psychologically hug yourself daily, the hugging of others is meaningless. Let me explain.

Low self-esteem runs from generation to generation. It is passed from parents to children just like genetic traits. According to Dr. William Glasser there are two basic human needs: the need to love and to be loved, and the need to feel worthwhile to ourselves and to others. Our health and happiness depend on receiving doses of both on a regular basis.

Where do you register on the love-yourself meter? On a scale of one to 10, how do you rate? If it's down at the bottom, change is the answer. One way to effect a turnaround is to start by helping others feel good about themselves. It will turn you away from the "me, me, gimme, gimme" philosophy that pervades our society. When you make others feel good, that, in turn, boosts your self-love meter.

These next few days are a wonderful time to put these thoughts into action. If you have no plans for the holidays, find a local homeless shelter and volunteer to spend time preparing and dishing out food. Find an association for abused and deprived children and give out hugs and teddy bears—guaranteed to warm your heart. If home is too stressful, get out and go to a nursing home. There are elderly folks who have no relatives. They'll welcome you with open arms and smile long after you have left.

GUS

It is Christmas Day and I know you are busy so I'll make this one short.

As a speaker I often visit churches. When I do, I usually give my lecture called "God, the Motivator Within."

God to some is still that white-haired, bearded old man who dwells in the heavens, lightning bolts in hand, ready to strike with doom, destruction and vengeance.

To others God has taken on a different persona. Reverend Helen Street calls him "Big Sweetie," giving him a softer, more modern image.

Children often imagine God looking like Casper the Ghost. They can laugh and enjoy this image. If it works for them that's great.

For me, I call him GUS—the Great Universal Spirit. It is a non-gender description and my theory is that GUS wants only good for me and those I love. When I speak to GUS I feel good inside and out. GUS fits my lifestyle easily and I feel quite in charge of my life knowing that GUS is always watching over me, compelling me to make the correct choices, easing my fears and worries, dissipating my guilt, ensuring my future will be rosy.

On this day, I invite all readers to find their own name for the Lord who resides within their spirit and give him or her a name. Find the essence of GUS within you and remember: Today is the best day of the rest of your life.

Wherever I Go, Ego!

I hope your holiday was a good one. We only have a few vignettes to go. If they have been helping you change for the better, that's good enough for me.

Whenever I lecture at seminars I am asked to pinpoint mankind's greatest problem. The answer I always give is the same: false ego.

As we grow older it becomes more difficult to dislodge the stubborn ego which has made a home inside ourselves. We hide behind it as though it were a brick wall. And for most of us it can become as hard and unyielding. The ego needs constant shoring up, or defending from those on the outside who try to knock it down with condemnation and criticism.

The only way to start dismantling a rigid ego is to take it apart brick by brick. Of course I have made an acronym designed to accomplish this task:

E: *Enthusiasm*
G: *Goals*
O: *Optimism*

The best way to tear down the wall of EGO is to let go of all negative energy and replace it with positive affirmations. For example, saying "I can't do this," should be substituted by "I can do this."

All it takes is practice, practice, practice to become ego-less.

Time for Review

For the next three days, I will reexamine some of the key ideas presented in this book.

Nearly 90 percent of us suffer from low self-esteem. This means most readers will benefit from some practical advice on how to turn that around.

When asked, most people said the following situations made them feel bad about themselves:

- Not having the money to pay bills
- Getting divorced
- Losing a job
- Being noticeably overweight
- Embarrassing oneself in public
- Being criticized by someone held in high esteem
- Doing something immoral

Interestingly enough, only the last one has anything to do with *self*esteem. The remaining problems have more to do with *external* forces, or the esteem of others toward you. This means you let the opinions of others govern how you feel about yourself!

The notion behind this book is to make you feel good no matter what. Nobody says you have to be thin as a rail to like yourself. If you are overweight and feel comfortable, so much the better. If you embarrass yourself in public, stop beating up on yourself—we've all done it. These days if you've lost your job chances are it probably has more to do with corporate downsizing than your performance. There are other jobs, better jobs, or go into business for yourself as I did.

None of us are exempt from criticism. That's how people make themselves feel better. They boost their own fragile egos by putting others down.

Leo Tolstoy wrote: "I am always with myself, and it is I who am my tormentor." Well now is the time to stop tormenting yourself!

You may not always be able to control what you think, but you can develop a positive mental attitude. If you are the captain of your ship, take over now and navigate yourself into the Sea of Confidence.

"You get the best out of others, when you give the best of yourself."

HARVEY FIRESTONE

"It is foolish to wait for your ship to come in unless you have sent one out."

ALFRED A. MONTAPERT

"Your peers won't care how much you know, until they know how much you care."

ANONYMOUS

Love and Positive Thinking

The connection is being made between love and positive thinking. I am not referring to physical love which is so prevalent in the movies, television and the media. I mean the old-fashioned kind between two people on an intimate level.

We have already dealt with the fact that you cannot love others until you love yourself. For example: Would you cook a meal that tastes nasty and serve it? Would you expect those eating it to like it? The same goes for you!

If you are bitter and filled with rage, how can you expect someone to love you? How can you love someone else with all that nasty garbage in the way? You cannot give away what you do not have—in this case love for yourself and for others.

Dr. Karl Menninger says: "Love cures people. Both the ones who give it and the ones who receive it." The trick is to have it so you can impart it to others.

"God loves you whether you like it or not," says a popular bumper sticker. This is known as unconditional love, the kind parents should have for their children and lovers should share with each other. Most important, unconditional love is the love you must have for yourself in order to truly enjoy life.

True love begins from *within*. Start looking for it today; find the seed and nourish it. It's not vanity, conceit or narcissism.

Self-love is the key to positive living and the enjoyment of life.

What I Have Learned

I have finally developed a philosophy I can live by and I'd like to share the major premises with you.

1. Our body mirrors the patterns of pessimistic thoughts and translates them into sickness and even death. Try to focus on the positive and eliminate the negative.
2. Condemnation, criticism and guilt do the most damage to our health. Condemnation and criticism are used to build our fragile egos by tearing down the self-esteem of others. This leads to guilt, the ultimate self-defeater.
3. Thoughts can be controlled and changed. If destructive thoughts creep in, immediately dispel them, thus keeping a healthy mindset.
4. Everyone suffers from guilt and self-hatred to some degree. To what degree are you culpable? Turn the self-hate into self-praise.
5. We are fully responsible for our own lives. The universe operates on the principles of cause and effect. Break the natural laws and you pay a price. Some call this the Law of Karma. Whatever the name, what goes around, comes around.
6. The only power you wield is in the present. Today is all there is, so nurture it carefully. There is no yesterday since you cannot retreat to the past. There is no tomorrow, that will come soon enough. Enjoy the moment. Seize the day. *Carpe Diem!*
7. When we learn to love ourselves, everything in life works with synergy. Self-love helps eliminate anger, despair and melancholy. Life is rosier. It will allow you to *"bloom where you are planted."*
8. Actions speak louder than words. Although you may know all of the above, put these principles into motion. But be careful not to mistake activity for achievement. Looking busy while repeating old acts is a waste of time and energy. Advance cautiously at first until you get the hang of it, then speed up and stay on course.

Happy New Year and good luck. I leave you with this thought from Galileo Galilei:

"You cannot teach a man anything.
You can only help him discover it within himself!"

"Each one has a mission to fulfill, a mission of love. At the hour of death when we come face to face with God, we are going to be judged on love; not on how much we have done, but how much love we have put into our actions."

MOTHER TERESA

"Once you have learned to love, you have learned to live."

WALTER M. GERMAIN

About the Author

Jacques Wiesel is a professional speaker and the author of several books and audio discs on self-improvement and self-inspiration. A former president of the New York Metro Chapter of the National Speakers Association, Wiesel has delivered keynote speeches and lead seminars on personal motivation, human resources development and management skills throughout the United States. He has been featured on numerous radio programs and hosted the television series *Positive Living*.

When Jacques was seven years old, his family fled Belgium in the face of Nazi invasion. Three years later, the Wiesel family arrived in the United States with nothing but their memories—of terror, homelessness and near-starvation. Jacques Wiesel overcame the negative mental attitudes that resulted from his childhood to become one of America's most enthusiastic and inspiring motivational speakers.

Photo Gallery

I'm at Limestone Air Force Base

I'm lecturing at City of Hope

My brother Irving & I in Naples' FL

My Mom & Dad in Williamsburg Brooklyn

My sister-in law Sumiko

My wife Carole & I on a cruise

*Photographer
Marc Gagnon & I*

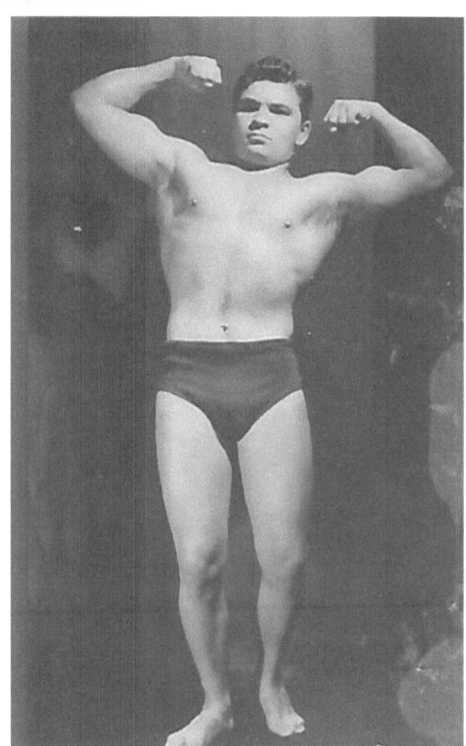

*When I worked out at
the YMHA NYC*

Im in China Town, NY selling World Book

Jacques & his service club crew in Carswell AFB TX

Jacques and his new BPW Group

My brother Irv (upper left) as tank commader in Korea

My mom & dad during Passover in the Catskills, NY

Carol Morris paints Jacques pictures of the Holocaust

My aunt Goldie & Cousins

My brother Irv plays Santa in Japan for US Troops

*My grandchildrem
Annelise & Zachary
Aug. 2018*

*Grandson's Logan &
Matthew 2017*

Our Flordia Family 2017

Our Indiana Family 2017

www.ingramcontent.com/pod-product-compliance
Lightning Source LLC
Chambersburg PA
CBHW030106100526
44591CB00009B/296